A NEW
CLIMATE
FOR THEOLOGY

A NEW
CLIMATE
FOR THEOLOGY

God,

the World, and

Global Warming

SALLIE McFAGUE

FORTRESS PRESS
Minneapolis

A New Climate for Theology
God, the World, and Global Warming

Scripture quotations, unless otherwise marked, are from the New Revised Standard
Version Bible, copyright © 1989 by the Division of Christian Education of the
National Council of Churches of Christ in the USA. Used by permission. All rights
reserved.

Cover images: copyright © Photodisc / Getty Images
Cover design: Paul Boenke, Eileen Engebretson, and John Goodman
Book design: Jessica A. Puckett

Library of Congress Cataloging-in-Publication Data
ISBN 978–0–8006–6271–4
McFague, Sallie.
  A new climate for theology : God, the world, and global warming / Sallie
McFague.
    p. cm.
  ISBN-13: 978–0–8006–6271–4 (alk. paper)
  1. Global warming—Religious aspects—Christianity. I. Title.
  BR115.G58M34 2008
  261.8'8—dc22   2007047973

The paper used in this publication meets the minimum requirements of American
National Standard for Information Sciences—Permanence of Paper for Printed
Library Materials, ANSI Z329.48-1984.

Manufactured in the U.S.A.

CONTENTS

To my granddaughters Natalie and Evelyn,
who must live in the world we leave them

INTRODUCTION

The recent awakening to the threat of climate change, epitomized by the 2007 United Nations report from the Intergovernmental Panel on Climate Change, is deep and widespread. The shock of realizing that our high-energy consumer lifestyle is sending the earth into potential disaster is a wake-up call. We are approaching the tipping point in global temperature that will change the basic conditions for the flourishing of life. We react in horror to the destruction and death we are bringing on the planet; we say, "No! This need not, must not happen."

Like many other people, I want to do something about it. I am a Christian theologian; therefore, the task for me is to ask what role theology plays in our "no" to the consequences of global warming. For the past eight years since I wrote *Life Abundant*, I have not known what to do next. In the epilogue to that book, I expressed dismay that the mainline churches are still focused on narrow issues of personal and, for the most part, sexual morality. Homosexuality commands most of the attention. But are these the most pressing issues of our time? As important as sexual issues are, should Christian theologians focus on them at the outset of the twenty-first century? Are there not other issues? Is there not, in fact, another vision of life on earth—a vision that we are called to articulate? Is our planet not in dire straits, and must we not acknowledge this reality and attempt to address it? Is climate change not bringing to a head the issues of justice and sustainability that demand a conversion from our greedy consumer-oriented culture to a vision in which all creatures might flourish? I close *Life Abundant* with the suggestion that the central vision of Christianity demands that we wake up to the destabilizing character of this faith—its insistence, its "wild" notion—that all are invited to the banquet of life.

Is there any hope for us—we middle-class North American Christians? Can we at least be honest, if not good? It might help if we could keep our "wild space" intact. Being a Christian, even a middle-class North American one—as I envision it—involves having a wild space. That wild space is the shocking suggestion—even if only a suspicion—that all really are invited to the banquet, that every creature deserves a place at the table. This is not the hegemonic view of our society or of the church: it is counter-cultural and counter-church. It is a different vision of the good life, but wild as it may seem, it is not necessarily wrong or impossible. Its two key principles are mundane ones: justice and sustainability. Could the wild space become the whole space—the household of planet earth where each of us takes only our share, cleans up after ourselves, and keeps the house in good repair for future dwellers? I do not know, but perhaps we Christians could at least admit what life abundant truly should be, terrifying as it may be.[1]

And here we are eight years later, facing a vision of dystopia from global warming that is as far removed as possible from what we want: the vision of the banquet where all are invited to the table, the abundant life of justice and sustainability, the deep desire within each of us—our wild space—that tells us a different world is possible. So what is the "next" thing I must do as a theologian? I want to suggest that theology within the context of climate change must focus on deconstructing and reconstructing two key doctrines: who we are and who God is. The interpretation of the God-world relationship is a critical issue. If theologians, who are some of the keepers and interpreters of this deep knowledge, allow false, inappropriate, unhelpful, and dangerous notions of God and ourselves to continue as our society's assumptions, we are not doing our job. A primary task of theologians is to guard and encourage right thinking about God and ourselves. This, of course, is but one small task needed for the planetary agenda to change. Other people—doctors, car manufacturers, teachers, parents, corporate leaders, lawyers, politicians, agriculturalists, and so on—also have important offerings to make in our struggle against climate change. The particular task of theologians is prior to our action; it is at its roots. It is a limited task and mainly a linguistic one: suggesting different language for talking about God and ourselves—with the hope that different action may follow. The limitations of this task and its possibilities are perhaps best seen in the negative: if we do not change our basic assumptions about God and ourselves from an individualistic to a communitarian view, can we expect people to change their behavior? If we know nothing else, do we have a choice?

Given this assignment, I begin in part one with the science of global warming, followed by a chapter on its significance for theology. These two chapters provide the groundwork for the rest of the book. It is critical, I believe, that theology be done within the contemporary scientific worldview; therefore, a careful reading of our empirical situation is the necessary beginning point. It is also important, I think, for theology to attend to the specific task for which it is responsible: *theos-logia*, words about God. To many people, it is not obvious that theology has anything to do with issues such as climate change. Why should it? My answer in chapter 2 is that theology must deal with global warming because one of the basic marks of the church is its ecological catholicity, which must be lived out in a political context. In other words, Christian faith is concerned with a just and sustainable existence for all of God's creation.

Having laid out the contemporary situation we face and theology's role in that situation, we turn in part two to the heart of the matter: Who are we? Who is God? How shall we live? Global warming is the coming to a head of the "ecological turn" that has been part of postmodernity at its best. A vision of the abundant life on planet Earth based on this turn, and the consequent reformulations of the doctrines of human being and of God, has been occurring for the last half century. This vision is widespread in ecofeminism and in process thought, in indigenous peoples' thinking and in liberation theologies, and in many other places. It has also been central to my own work. Climate change names this ecological turn in a negative and frightening way: it tells us loud and clear that our conventional consumer-culture anthropology is false. It also warns Christians that a supernatural, transcendent God is neither faithful to the tradition's incarnationalism nor relevant for our times. Therefore, these central chapters—3, 4, and 5—on ourselves, God, and life in our world are the distillation of my theological work since *Life Abundant*, brought to a head by climate change. What they say is that global warming is the empirical evidence that different ways of envisioning ourselves and God are necessary.

Part three focuses on two current challenges for climate change and the sort of theology I am proposing: service to God and urban ecology. What would the worship of God and service to our neighbor look like in a postmodern, climate-change context? Deconstruction, the literary and philosophical movement associated with Jacques Derrida, puts severe limits on God-talk of any sort, conventional or reconstructive. Would a theology that praises God and has compassion toward others be credible in postmodern thought? Does deconstruction's suspicion of the hidden idolatry and fundamentalism in religious language extend to all theology? Would a sacramental, prophetic theology be permitted, one that sees the glory of God in the world and practices limitation and sacrifice so that others might live? Chapter 6 attempts to make the case that a minimalist theology focusing on praise and compassion would be acceptable to deconstruction as well as sufficient for our context of climate change. Similarly, in chapter 7, we look at another challenge to climate change—the insatiable energy appetite of cities. What kind of theology would be appropriate to deal with the huge energy needs and wants of twenty-first-century cities with populations of twelve million or more? Again, our views of who we are and who God is come into play. The sacramental and prophetic religious impulses that limit God-talk to signs of God in the world and that limit our own use of the world's resources are key insights for a theology of climate change for cities.

Finally, in part four we address the most difficult of all climate change issues: despair and hope. Given the dystopia we may well be facing, we ask in chapter 8 how a different world, one of justice and sustainability for human beings and the planet, is possible. We ask whether our wild space, the longing in each of us for a better world, is just a fantasy, an ungrounded hope. And we consider the necessity of facing reality and not shying away from what science is telling us about the future. Finally, in the last chapter, we press the issue of despair and hope to its foundations—what, if anything, can we hope for? Throughout these concluding chapters we deepen the relationship between God and the world that has been emerging throughout the book: the realization that we live and move and have our being in God. The world is enclosed within God: God is always present in and for the world. Our task is to awaken to and acknowledge who we are: we are reflections of the divine, as is all creation. We are not alone: we live in God along with all other forms of life. Our hope is therefore not in ourselves, but in the words of Gerard Manley Hopkins, "because the Holy Ghost over the bent world broods with warm breast and with ah! bright wings."[2]

In conclusion, Christian theology is the attempt to think about God and the world—who God is and who we are—in light of what the tradition has claimed in the past and what we must say in the present. Every Christian is a theologian; each of us has a theology. That is, each of us has a picture, a set of assumptions, usually not conscious, of how we think God and the world are related. And all of us can and do express through our words and actions who we think God is and who we think we are. These unconscious or implicit theologies are very powerful. They control many of our decisions and actions; we rely on them as justification for what we do personally and as a nation. Theology matters.

Those two words sum up my reason for writing this book. Theology is certainly not the only thing that matters in regard to climate change, but it does play a part. It helps us question our maneuvers of denial and attempts at self-justification. It also gives us permission and/or the obligation to act in very different ways, depending on our assumptions about God and ourselves. Theology matters.

PART ONE

*The **Science** and*
Its Significance
*for **Theology***

1

CLIMATE CHANGE: The EVIDENCE and CONSEQUENCES

Warming of the climate system is unequivocal, as is now evident from observations of increases in global average air and ocean temperatures, widespread melting of snow and ice, and rising global mean sea level.
  —Fourth Assessment Report, United Nations Intergovernmental Panel on Climate Change, February 2007

Overcoming Denial

In his book on global warming, *An Inconvenient Truth*, Al Gore quotes Winston Churchill: "The era of procrastination, of half measures, of soothing and baffling expedients, of delays, is coming to its close. In its place we are entering a period of consequences."[1] Churchill wrote these words in 1936 with a storm gathering in continental Europe that would have unprecedented consequences, culminating in the Jewish

Holocaust. People on both sides of the Atlantic did not want to believe it: denial was deep and broad.

We are facing another such time, one of equal if not greater danger to human beings and our planet.[2] But in the case of climate change, the evidence is even clearer than was the Nazi threat in 1936. In February 2007, the United Nations Intergovernmental Panel on Climate Change (IPCC) issued the first part of its Fourth Assessment Report: "The Physical Science Basis," with two more parts to follow on consequences and mitigation efforts.[3] In this report, the overall assessment is "unequivocal" confidence that global warming is under way, and "very high confidence" (90 percent) that human activities are the cause. The main points elaborating on this judgment are as follows:

1. The "greenhouse" gases—carbon dioxide, methane, and nitrous oxide—have increased substantially since the Industrial Revolution (1750) and now far exceed pre-industrial concentrations.
2. The global increase in carbon dioxide is due mainly to fossil fuel use.
3. The concentration of carbon dioxide in the earth's atmosphere "exceeds by far the natural carbon range" over the last 650,000 years.
4. Many long-term changes in climate change have been observed at global, continental, and regional levels, including Arctic temperatures and ice as well as ocean salinity and wind patterns, resulting in "extreme weather including droughts, heavy precipitation, heat waves, and the intensity of tropic cyclones."
5. Hotter temperatures and rises in the sea level will "continue for centuries," regardless how much humans reduce their carbon emissions, and it is "very likely" (90 percent) that heat waves, droughts, and extreme weather will become more frequent.
6. The IPCC projects a possible global temperature rise of up to 6°C by 2100, with its best estimate a 4.5°C increase during this century.

This conclusion may seem benign on the surface—4.5°C doesn't sound very significant. However, when we recall that during the last ice age the global temperature was only 5°C cooler than now, we realize the difference that a small increase or decrease in global temperature can make. Moreover, the IPCC is a conservative organization. It reports the consensus view of hundreds of scientists who study articles on climate change published in peer-reviewed journals. It does not conduct its own research but assesses all of the science on climate change considered credible by the world's scientists. Australian scientist Tim Flannery notes in his book *The Weather Makers* that the IPCC report is "very conservative":

> The outcome is that the pronouncements of the IPCC do not represent mainstream science, nor even good science, but lowest common denominator science—and of course delivered at glacial speed. Yet in spite of its faults, the IPCC's assessment reports, which are issued every five years, carry weight with the media and government precisely because they represent a consensus view. If the IPCC says something, you had better believe it—and then allow for the likelihood that things are far worse than it says they are.[4]

It is necessary to underline this statement because climate change deniers continue to exist. To the degree that any scientific knowledge is reliable, the work on climate change is. As Al Gore notes, in a study of 928 articles on climate change appearing in peer-reviewed journals, none cast doubt on global warming.[5] However, in articles on the subject appearing in the popular press, 53 percent claimed there were "two sides" to the issue. It is understandable why many people doubt the science, given the propensity of the media to create a conflict for the sake of reader interest. However, in light of the IPCC's recent report, such skepticism is irresponsible. The first step in dealing with a major planetary crisis, as Churchill reminded us in 1936, is to overcome denial. As Donald Kennedy, editor in chief of *Science*, has said, "Consensus as strong as the one that has developed around this topic [climate change] is rare in science."[6]

Since the publication of the IPCC report, the 2007 Nobel Peace Prize has been awarded to Al Gore and the IPCC committee. This is a stunning witness to the seriousness of climate change: it is, the committee suggests, a matter of "war and peace." In the words of the award, it was given to those fighting global warming because "greater competition for the earth's resources" could result in "increased danger of violent conflicts and wars, within and between states."[7] Climate change is now an issue of human—indeed, of planetary—security. It is a more total and permanent threat to security than the so-called war on terror. Moreover, the final Synthesis Report of the IPCC issued in November 2007, paints an even grimmer picture than did the February 2007 release, with more Arctic ice melting and greater emphasis on immediate, world-wide action. [8] Why, then, are we hesitating? What more do we need to know in order to respond as people did in World War II?

One reason for resistance may be ignorance—not ignorance that climate change is occurring, but ignorance of what its consequences will be. Future scenarios often focus on particular events in particular places on the planet—cyclones, droughts, flooding, food shortages, melting glaciers. These occurrences sound disturbing, but many people suppose either that they personally will escape the worst forecasts or that scientific know-how will save us as it has in the past. But the projected future is more ominous: it is not only particular extreme events from a gradual temperature rise, but rather a globally degraded environment for living things when temperatures reach the tipping point, the point at which the rise is irreversible. If temperatures were to rise gradually over the next century, allowing people, animals, and vegetation time to adjust, then a comparable gradual diminishment of greenhouse gases might be the appropriate action. But that is not what is happening. Already, according to the IPCC Fourth Assessment Report, the *rate* of temperature increase on our planet since the Industrial Revolution is unprecedented. Once temperature increases reach a certain level, a disturbing phenomenon occurs: positive feedback. James Lovelock describes it in these words:

> What makes global warming so serious and so urgent is that the great Earth system, Gaia, is trapped in a vicious circle of positive feedback. Extra heat, from any source, whether from greenhouse gases, the disappearance of the Arctic ice or the Amazon forest, is amplified, and its effects are more than additive. It is almost as if we lit a fire to keep warm, and failed to notice, as we piled on the fuel, that the fire was out of control and the furniture ignited. When that happens, little time is left to put out the fire. Global warming, like a fire, is accelerating and almost no time is left to act. [9]

Scientists are especially concerned that positive feedback is causing the melting of Arctic ice to accelerate at a tailspin rate, with far-reaching effects on the climate of North America and Europe. The process works like a loop, with warmer temperatures and melting reinforcing each other. Snow and ice reflect sunlight and reduce global warming, but when ice begins to melt, more open water appears. Whereas ice reflects incoming solar radiation like a mirror, hence stabilizing temperature, the open sea absorbs heat. As the water warms up, it puts even more pressure on the edge of ice adjacent to it, hence contributing to a faster melting rate. Each year, the pace of melting quickens and will eventually reach the tipping point at which the remaining ice collapses under the explosive melt. Rapid melting of huge ice masses will cause the sea to rise several meters, flooding islands and low-lying coastal areas. A recent dramatic announcement made by the U.S. National Ice Center illustrates the seriousness of this concern: "Northwest Passage is wide open for shipping." The fabled polar shipping route was almost completely clear of ice in August 2007—an unprecedented event. As the scientists point out, this means that next year's melt season will begin with a much-reduced base of ice, thus speeding up the process toward the time when the entire polar region, including the North Pole, would be ice free in the summer. That time is now predicted to be 2030.[10]

Since the publication of the 2007 IPCC report, the news media has been full of studies suggesting that positive feedback appears to be stronger and faster than expected. For example, a recent study claims that the capacity of the earth's carbon sinks—its oceans and lands—to absorb greenhouse gases is diminishing, raising the probability that global warming will occur more rapidly and dramatically than reported by the IPCC. As the oceans and lands respond to global warming, they in turn can absorb less heat, thus contributing to greater climate forcing. As one of the researchers remarked, "It's a positive feedback whereby sinks appear to be responding to global warming in a way that increases global warming. It's not good news."[11]

But most of us do not see an out-of-control climate when we wake up each morning to start our day. In many parts of the world, things seem fine. This is because there is a built-in delay before the dire consequences of global warming become evident. The climate system of the planet is large and tough, able to take a lot; if it were not, it would be changing all the time. "Over the past two million years, even as the temperature of the earth has swung wildly, it has always remained within certain limits. The planet has often been colder than today, but rarely warmer, and then only slightly."[12] Hence, the self-reinforcing warming process that we humans have set in motion since the Industrial Revolution is a rare and profound event, especially in its rapidity of change. However, its effects are not immediate—and thus we have difficulty seeing the urgency for action. Even if greenhouse gases were held steady at today's levels, the full effect of our emissions would not become evident for several decades. This is because the whole system, the entire planetary climate, must heat up in all its parts—warming the air and the surface of the land, melting sea ice and glaciers, and, most important, heating up the oceans—a complex and uneven process.[13] Elizabeth Kolbert makes a chilling comment on this fact: "The delay that is built into the system is, in a certain sense, fortunate. It enables us, with the help of climate models, to foresee what is coming and therefore to prepare for it. But in another sense it is clearly disastrous, because it allows us to keep adding CO_2 to the atmosphere while fobbing the impacts off on our children and grandchildren."[14]

Kolbert's remark helps to unmask the strange dilemma that global warming presents: for a long time things will be fine, but then, suddenly, perhaps within a decade or two, it will be too late.[15] Once a significant warming event has started, such as the melting of the Greenland or the West Antarctic ice sheet, it is irreversible. We are not used to such a scenario—a catastrophe, with built-in delays, that tips suddenly. It has been compared to playing in a rowboat. "You can tip it and just go back. And then you tip it and you get to the other stable state, which is upside down."[16] Since most of human history has taken place during a relatively steady-state climate, we continue to deny that immediate and profound changes in our behavior are necessary. However, the nature of this phenomenon, global warming, is such that we cannot wait until the evidence is certain. The 2007 IPCC Fourth Assessment Report is telling us that the evidence of global warming is "unequivocal." If we then understand and accept the peculiar character of global warming— that once warming begins it is self-reinforcing and inevitable—action becomes imperative.

Climate is our planet's largest, most important, and most vulnerable interlocking system: it allows for and sustains life. Destablizations have consequences; we cannot allow massive changes to take place and believe we can carry on with our lives as usual. Therefore, a sober, prudent assessment of our situation behooves us to take action now. It is not apocalyptic or radical to do so, but simply common sense. We insure our homes, our cars, and our own bodies on slighter evidence that they will meet with disaster. How then can we turn from the threat of climate change as less plausible, less important?

Climate change, quite simply, is the issue of the twenty-first century. It is not one issue among many, but, like the canary in the mine, it is warning us that the way we are living on our planet is causing us to head for disaster. We must change. All of the other issues we care about—social justice, peace, prosperity, freedom—cannot occur unless our planet is healthy. It is the unifying issue of our time; it is our "World War II," as it were: the concern that must develop into a worldwide movement for change of mind and change of action.

Internalizing Vulnerability

A radically different understanding of ourselves is necessary. Climate change is making us realize how profoundly dependent we are on the health of our planet, graphically illustrated by each breath of air we take. In a powerful description of our total dependence on the atmosphere, the great aerial ocean that regulates the planet's temperature and connects everything with everything else, Tim Flannery raises our consciousness:

> It is in our lungs that we connect to our Earth's great aerial bloodstream, and in this way the atmosphere inspires us from our first breath to our last. The time-honoured custom of slapping newborns on the bottom to elicit a drawing of breath, and the holding of a mirror to the lips of the dying are bookmarks of our existence. And it is the atmosphere's oxygen that sparks our inner fire, permitting us to move, eat and reproduce—indeed to live. Clean, fresh air gulped straight from the great aerial ocean is not just an old-fashioned tonic for human health, it is life itself, and 13.5 kilograms of it are required by every adult, every day of their lives.[17]

We should tack a copy of this quotation to our bathroom mirrors, to be read slowly every morning.

In order to begin to act differently, we must submerge ourselves in a different view of who we are. We can begin to do this by noticing our own breath, the taking in of life-giving oxygen second by second by second as we traverse the time, whether short or long, between our birth and our death. What we do during our lives, who we become and what we accomplish—all of this depends on the simple, continuous act of breathing. We must begin to reflect upon ourselves from the perspective of the basics, not in terms of our "additions." We must consider what allows us to exist in the first place, not what we can accomplish. This exercise is similar to what alcoholics realize when they "bottom out," acknowledging that they have no control over their lives and must "let go and let God" (in Twelve Step parlance). In a related move, we addicts of the high-consumption lifestyle that is changing the very composition of the air we breathe must let go of our greedy, controlling practices and respect the real basis of our existence, earth's atmosphere.

Once we make this fundamental move, we open ourselves to understanding our dilemma in a new way. We begin to see how the interlocking systems of our planet are changing under the weight of the human population and its desired lifestyle. Our minds become available to accept an interpretation of our world that is dramatically different from the modern, individualistic picture of human beings as superior to—possessing and controlling—the rest of nature.

A few examples of our strange new weather can serve as wake-up calls for moving to a different picture of ourselves. We who have become accustomed to assuming that the "weather" is a safe subject for casual conversation, with its comfortable rhythm of the seasons and the expectation of snow in winter and rain in the spring, are in for a shock. The "new weather" may be nothing like this; in fact, one of its features that we have noted is its *unpredictability*. Flannery states that "in response to heating or cooling, for example, our atmosphere can at once transform itself from one climatic state into something quite different. This allows storms, droughts, floods or wind patterns to alter on a global level, and to do so more or less at the same time.[18]

Thus, global warming can change the climate in jerks, jumping from one stable state to another, as with the rowboat example. This is one of the most shocking wake-up calls we can imagine, for it means that the system that is the unacknowledged, taken-for-granted basis of our lives in all its facets—physical, emotional, cultural, economic— cannot be counted on. The jerky, unstable, unpredictable character of the weather means that we cannot continue with "business as usual."

Another wake-up call is the earth's melting ice. The Himalayan Glaciers, among the most affected by global warming, "contain 100 times as much ice as the Alps and provide more than half of the drinking water for 40 percent of the world's population—through seven Asian river systems that all originate on the same plateau."[19] The consequences of their melting—the serious depletion of drinking water for 40 percent of the earth's population—are staggering. Or consider the Siberian permafrost, frozen since the last ice age but now melting. This area of tundra contains seventy billion tons of stored carbon, which is becoming unstable as the permafrost melts. The carbon in these Siberian soils is ten times the amount emitted annually from human-generated sources.[20] What is projected here is an ecological landslide of mammoth proportions. We need to use our imaginations to project what dramatically different weather means in concrete cases.

These wake-up calls illustrate that we have entered a time when the world will be different from the one we have known. It is not simply that droughts, storms, heat waves, and hurricanes will become more frequent. Rather, it is that we are close to the tipping point of radical change that will have consequences for the way we eat and work, travel and conduct business, raise our children, practice medicine and law, build cities, grow our food, and so on. The radical unpredictability of earth's climate is new information to most people. The weather used to be something you could count on: there might be an unusually hot summer or an exceptionally cold winter, but these were anomalies in an otherwise trustworthy pattern. This meant that at the deepest unconscious level, we could "count on" the climate—that is, on the atmosphere that is the basis of all life. We humans may have seldom thought of the weather this way—as the ground of existence—but nonetheless that assumed confidence infiltrated our sense of security at a very basic level. If it is now possible—indeed probable—as the best science is telling us that climate unpredictability, runaway heat, uncontrolled melting, and other dire events lie in our future, how can we any longer count on "life as we have known it"? The answer is that we cannot, and this is the truth we must face up to.

The scientists are not saying that it is inevitable that we will irreparably damage the climate that nurtures life on our planet—but it is possible, and probable, if we do not take action. Our situation is similar to predictions that the Allies would lose the Second World War unless they mobilized all of their efforts toward stopping the rising fascist menace. In the case of climate change, however, the relationship between cause and effect is not as clear as it is in a war. As George Monbiot points out, the relationship "seems so improbable." "By turning on the lights, filling the kettle, taking the children to school, driving to the shops, we are condemning other people to death. We perform these acts without passion or intent. Many of those things we have understood to be good—even morally necessary—must now be seen as bad."[21]

One of the best illustrations of this new reversal of what is "good" and "bad" is aviation travel. A single return flight between New York and London produces 1.2 tons of greenhouse gases per passenger, the equivalent of a year's allowable emissions if emissions were rationed fairly among all of the planet's human beings.[22] In discussing "the distance [we] must travel to visit friends and partners and relatives on the other side of the planet," Monbiot notes that "love miles" may be our undoing: "The world could be destroyed by love."[23] Many people who would not drive, let alone own, an SUV think nothing of flying all over the world for pleasure or business or even to attend conferences on global warming! It appears that one of the lifestyle changes that middle-class humans worldwide must make is a severe limitation on air travel. Such a cutback will, of course, drastically change life as we know it. However, "life as we know it" is a very recent phenomenon and, in any case, is available only to a small percentage of the world's population. Monbiot reminds us that the world we "know" and take for granted is only approximately fifty years old and is only for people "like us." It took a leap of imagination to conceive that people might fly long distances, that it was possible for many people to do so, and that it was possible for *you* and *me* to do so. Fifty years ago, no one thought of shopping in New York if you lived in Europe—it was not "natural" or "necessary" to do so. As Monbiot points out, since we constructed the alternative world of the twentieth century with its high-consumption travel, we also can construct another alternative world with low-consumption travel.[24]

Air travel raises another issue, a moral one: How can we be so presumptuous as to insist that simply because we privileged human beings have "grown accustomed" to unlimited plane travel, it is our "right" even if it means the degradation of earth's atmosphere so that poorer human beings and other life-forms must suffer the consequences? Aviation, for those who can afford it, now becomes a moral issue. As we begin to realize the universality, complexity, and vulnerability of the atmosphere, climate change takes on a new urgency. We must reduce the number, length, and speed of all forms of travel, using other technology, such as the Internet, to communicate globally. We must begin to imagine how we can live in an alternative world to the one modernity has constructed. A postmodern world will be different—not necessarily a less happy one for human beings, but certainly one in which people, especially people like us, must find abundant life without consuming so much. Al Gore illustrates this point when he compares the effects of new versus old technology:

> Old habits plus old technology equals Predictable Consequences
>
> Old habits plus new technology equals Dramatically Altered Consequences[25]

Our old travel habits when confined to walking, bicycles, horses, ships, and trains resulted in considerably less carbon dioxide emissions than when linked to cars and planes. We have not changed our desire and intention to move around the world, limited only by our ability to pay; what has changed is the technology that moves us, resulting in energy expenditures at a drastically different level. We see the same pattern in warfare conducted with bows and arrows, muskets and rifles, versus contemporary weapons technology and levels, not to mention nuclear bombs. War is no longer soldiers with rifles fighting each other; now it is wholesale demolition of cities and citizens. Travel is no longer the occasional movement of people to new places with the help of legs, wind, and steam; now it is the daily commute of millions from home to work by car and the limitless use of air travel for all who desire and can pay for it. *We cannot continue to live as we have in the past in the world we have created. We have created these new conditions, and now we must learn to live within them.*

This should not be impossible to do. Think back, if you are fifty years old or older—or imagine, if you are younger—to a time when people had small houses, one bathroom, maybe a family car, minimal electronic equipment (a radio, a TV), walked to school, took the subway or train to work, and traveled by plane perhaps once a year. We will not return to such a time, nor am I suggesting we try to do so. This memory or imaginative exercise is only to illustrate that we *can* live differently and not be unhappy. A widely known statistic is that Americans have never been happier than they were in 1957—when many had the lifestyle described above (or the chance at it) and before rampant consumption became the dominant lifestyle.[26] Once we get over the paralysis of believing that a different world is necessarily a worse one, we can free our imaginations to construct a different and perhaps a better world—one in which sustainability and the just distribution of resources for all of the earth's inhabitants will be priorities. We must accommodate our picture of the good life to fit within the earth's economy, for unless we do so, there can be no good life for any of us.

> In effect, 1986 marks the year that humans reached Earth's carrying capacity, and ever since we have been running the environmental equivalent of a deficit budget, which is only sustained by plundering our capital base. The plundering takes the form of overexploiting fisheries, overgrazing pasture until it becomes desert, destroying forests, and polluting our oceans and atmosphere, which in turn leads to the large number of environmental issues we face. In the end, though, the environmental budget is the only one that really counts.[27]

Facing Consequences

The consequences of global warming are no longer in doubt. This is the conclusion of the second section of the 2007 IPCC Fourth Assessment Report, titled "Climate Change Impacts, Adaptation and Vulnerability," which evaluates the impact of climate change on different parts of the world.[28] As British scientist Michael Perry, one of the authors, comments, "For the first time we are no longer arm-waving with models, [speculating that] this might happen. This is what you call empirical information, on the ground. We can measure it."[29] Moreover, the consequences will be unjust. North America and Western Europe have contributed two-thirds of carbon dioxide emissions, while only 3 percent has come from Africa. However, the northern, richer countries will suffer fewer adverse consequences, and they are also better able to pay for expensive adaptive measures to reduce the impact. These countries are already turning seawater into drinking water, erecting flood barriers, cultivating genetically altered drought-resistant seeds. Nothing of the sort is happening in Africa and in similar high-risk areas. Yale economist Robert O. Mendelsohn notes in relation to the IPCC's conclusions, "The original idea was that we were all in this together, and that was an easier idea to sell. But the research is not supporting that. We're not in it together."[30] This conclusion might appear to undercut the sense that we must take unified action in order to curb greenhouse gases. A chink has now appeared in the wall, and it will be very tempting for large, industrialized countries in northern climates to focus on insulating themselves against the worst effects, at least for the next generation or so. As Rajendra Pachauri, the chairman of the IPCC, remarks, "The inequity of this whole situation is really enormous if you look at who's responsible and who's suffering as a result."[31] In even sharper words, Henry I. Miller of Stanford University adds, "Like the sinking of the Titanic, catastrophes are not democratic. A much higher fraction of passengers from the cheaper decks were lost. We'll see the same phenomenon with global warming."[32] Even China, which has recently surpassed the United States in annual carbon dioxide emissions, nonetheless has contributed to date only 8 percent since 1850, whereas 56 percent has come from the Western countries.[33] Therefore, as a growing company of developing countries and environmental lawyers insist, the first world owes a climate debt to the third world. As Pachauri comments, "It's the poorest of the poor in the world, and this includes poor people even in prosperous societies, who are going to be the worst hit. This does become a global responsibility in my view."[34]

Hence, although it may be possible for the first world to focus on adaptive measures to protect itself in the near future, it is neither just to do so nor rational in the long run since giants such as China and India are quickly becoming major emissions polluters. Thus, we Westerners must "face the consequences" not only for ourselves, but also for the others, especially the poorest and most vulnerable, who will suffer from our profligate consumerism. The climate change scenario is similar to other situations in which the rich and the poor experience vastly different life possibilities and outcomes. It is surely no accident that the same anthropology that fuels market capitalism—the insatiable desires of the individual—is emerging in climate change, the twenty-first century's most serious crisis. It is another piece of evidence that this anthropology is unjust and unsustainable. Unless we rethink our sense of humanity toward a radically communitarian view, we will once again fall into the lie of short-term individual benefit while ignoring the truth of our long-term and basic interrelationship and interdependence. In this regard, climate change is *not* like the sinking of the *Titanic*, for while the rich countries may fortify themselves for the short term, there is no permanent escape from our common fate—we all must breathe the same air.

So the stakes are higher than we thought. We must now, in addition to seeing ourselves in the common lot of humanity, realize that there are vast differences among human beings in terms of responsibility for the crisis as well as those suffering its consequences. The two groups are not identical. This realization underscores the inexorable connection between ecological and justice issues. The days are long gone when people who sounded the alarm about global warming were considered "green freaks" who ought rather be concerned with human poverty. We now recognize the overarching planetary totality in which all of us live, thus bringing issues of justice and sustainability under the same roof. But we also see the split that market capitalism has made—the split between the wealthy and the poor—in stark new terms. Not only do the poor of the world enjoy fewer benefits from consumerism, but now with climate change—one of the consequences of our consumerism—their very survival is at stake. They did not create the problem, but they will reap the consequences. The fact that we wealthy nations did not "intend" these consequences is not important. We are nonetheless responsible for both cutting our emissions drastically and helping the most affected countries lessen the blow with mitigating technology.

It used to be politically incorrect to speak of adaptation to global warming, since this terminology implies adjusting to it rather than eliminating it. We now know that we cannot eliminate it; at best, with all forces mobilized, we might be able to keep the temperature increase below 2°C over the next fifty years—and then hopefully maintain that level in the future. But, in the meantime and especially for our poorer brothers and sisters who did not cause this crisis, we need to develop and share mitigating strategies against famine, drought, floods, disease, and so on. We need to work on two fronts: reducing our emissions to keep them below the tipping point of catastrophe *and* sharing mitigating funds and technology with those who will experience the worst consequences. It is hard to imagine *not* doing these things: climate change is surely the most severe test we have ever faced, not only in regard to our own survival, but equally important, in regard to our "humanity." It is for this reason that "who we think we are" becomes of critical importance.

Contemplating Action

If we have reached the point where we have overcome denial of climate change, internalized our vulnerability to its effects, and recognized our particular responsibility for its consequences, perhaps we are now ready for the big leap: taking action. In Churchill's words, "the era of procrastination, of half measures, of soothing and baffling expedients, of delays" is over. Perhaps we are ready to face the music.

But this is easier said than done. In fact, we do not even know what to do, for the problem is so all-encompassing, so global, so broad, and so deep that it invites paralysis, not action. As Flannery comments, "When we consider the fate of the planet as a whole, we must be under no illusions as to what is at stake. Earth's average temperature is around 15 degrees C., and whether we allow it to rise by a single degree, or 3 degrees C., will decide the fate of hundreds of thousands of species, and most probably billions of people."[35] Our first reaction after accepting climate change is despair: we are overwhelmed by the importance and immensity of what faces us. We are not up to it, we say. We wish we were still in denial, able to eat, sleep, and be merry, able to return to innocence and ignorance. But that is not possible. Once we have accepted and internalized the evidence of climate change, we are caught. We must act.

There are many levels at which action must take place. The third installment of the IPCC Fourth Assessment Report on climate change deals with mitigation policies for reducing and eventually stabilizing global greenhouse emissions. The good news from this study is that technology is available and the economics favorable for doing the task. That is, we know how to drastically reduce greenhouse gases, and the cost, if we were to do so immediately and globally, would be about 3 percent of the global GNP—not an outrageous figure.[36] The bad news is hidden in the qualifying phrase "if we were to do so immediately and globally." If all economic and governmental institutions worldwide were to take the necessary measures, through taxes and incentives to ensure lifestyle changes throughout all levels of the human population, the task could be accomplished. We could stabilize greenhouse gas emissions so as to keep the global temperature at approximately 2°C by the end of the century. In other words, climate change is not necessarily an apocalyptic event that will destroy human life and other life on our planet. We know what needs to be done, and we have the technology to do it. The third section of the 2007 IPCC report lays out specific mitigation technologies and practices currently available to reduce emissions in all sectors: energy supply, transport, buildings, industry, agriculture, forestry, and waste. Moreover, it suggests policies to realize these emission goals: regulations and standards, taxes, tradable permits, financial incentives, voluntary agreements, information instruments. Of course, it will be very difficult, complex, and messy to undertake this task, but it is not impossible.

The mitigation section of the report makes it absolutely clear that all levels of all societies must participate in *lowering emissions*, not just in trading or offsetting them. Already one sees the temptation of easy solutions emerging, such as paying a small fee to "offset" one's aviation or SUV emissions. Presumably the fees would plant trees in deforested areas or build clean power sources in developing countries. Thus, we first-world, well-off people could continue our energy-rich lifestyle with only a small fee to assuage our guilt. Not only are many such offset credits worthless, but they permit us to continue our irresponsible behavior—and to do so with an easy conscience.

The task ahead of us will take all of us working together with all that we have. The goal that we must reach—a stable global temperature with an increase of no more than 2°C—is so demanding, so serious, that it will take a coordinated global effort with the first world, the major polluter as well as the source of the needed technology and funding, leading the way. While some factions favor business incentives with others insisting that government regulation is the only path, the IPCC report recommends working on all fronts. As in the case of World War II, when government and business put aside their ideologies in order to mobilize all forces to win the war, such joint effort is necessary now. Global warming is not a contest between personal, business, and governmental levels to provide the solution: all are needed. To be sure, a smart emissions tax will encourage business to use its imagination to reduce emissions, with the result being more efficient cars, buildings, and forms of travel. Regulatory standards for electricity generation and for more efficient vehicles, buildings, and transit will also reduce our greenhouse emissions. And finally, individuals can reduce emissions by what they do in their personal lives—how they work, travel, eat, and play.

Behind all of these proposals for action at all levels is the problem hidden in the qualifying phrase "if we were to do so immediately and globally." *One critical issue is the motivation to act.* We must realize that the "problem" is in our heads and hearts as much as it is in the policies of governments and of multinational corporations. As Monbiot points out, "In fighting climate change, we must fight not only the oil companies, the airlines and the governments of the rich world; we must also fight ourselves."[37] *We* are the enemy: our beliefs about who we are and what we are entitled to are as much at fault as the institutions that control trade and make war. In fact, our beliefs and our institutions are secretly connected. As Monbiot notes, governments know that the electorate wants them to fail with regulatory measures, for otherwise we would have to change—and "we can contemplate a transformation of anyone's existence but our own."[38] It is this connection between the personal and the political that makes change so difficult, for in a democracy the basic beliefs of citizens ultimately control the actions of institutions, both business and government. A change of heart will not save the planet, but the interconnection of the personal and the political must be acknowledged. In this provocative statement by Monbiot, the connection is clear: "I am sorry to say that only regulation—that deeply unfashionable idea—can quell the destruction wrought by the god we serve, the god of our own appetites. Manmade global warming cannot be restrained unless we persuade the government to force us to change the way we live."[39] In reality, the connection is a circle: *governments must force us to change the way we live, but we must elect legislators who will create the necessary regulations.* In a curious fashion, we must acknowledge our weakness, our appetites, our greedy (sinful?) disposition to live wrongly and falsely on our planet in order to elect lawmakers who will help us to live better! Hence, the goal of climate change action is "to encourage people not only to change the way they live but also to force their governments to make such choices easier."[40] Thus, Monbiot claims, climate change "must become the world's most powerful political movement."[41]

It is between these two poles—the personal and the political—that important work needs to be done. It is not the only work that needs doing, for every activity people engage in must change—from how we grow food and make cars to how we educate our children and take vacations. But the particular passage from personal belief to corporate regulatory action is a critical one. It contains at least three steps. First, we need to analyze how we middle-class Western human beings view ourselves and our place on planet Earth. Second, we need to suggest a radically different paradigm for our place. Third, we need to incorporate this new view into our institutions. Only if our basic assumptions about human life and its place change and are embodied at the institutional level can we make the necessary paradigm shift in our thought and action. The problem is in our hearts and minds *and* in our laws and institutions: they influence each other in a delicate dance in which first one leads and then the other.

Two illustrations come to mind: first, the 1954 *Brown v. Board of Education* case before the United States Supreme Court, outlawing segregation in public schools. Many said at the time that hearts must change before action could occur, but, in fact, the sequence was considerably more complex. The law forced students to integrate, and over the next fifty years, changes occurred: while many segregated schools still exist (and some have even resegregated), the hearts and minds of the majority of white Americans have made progress toward appreciating equality in public facilities. Another example is the Canadian public health and educational systems. Both medical care and education are basically single-track in Canada (there is no large, separate private track for either). While Canadians rage against the inadequacies of both systems, they seem to realize the necessity of one track: in order for medical and educational services to be better for themselves, they must work for improvements in the entire system. They appear to want the government to help them retain a communitarian rather than an individualistic standard for human well-being. Hearts and minds need help to be better!

Thus, the dance between personal transformation and public regulation is necessary, with each allowing the other a turn at leading. We are facing a time when serious work needs to be done on both fronts: we must take a long, hard look at our picture of the human place on the planet, and we must mobilize as if for a world war to enact real lifestyle changes. The first of these tasks—the anthropological one—will be the focus of this book. Theologians and practitioners of religion have, I believe, a special responsibility for reflecting on the most basic assumptions about ourselves. Other cultural, societal, and intellectual fields of course do as well, so this task is a shared one. It is but one piece of the planetary agenda that climate change has set for the twenty-first century. When Monbiot considers governmental reluctance to spend money on climate change but a willingness to subsidize oil, coal, and other activities that lead to environmental destruction, he asks why "governments seem to find it so easy to raise the money to wreck the biosphere and so difficult to raise the money required to save it."[42] The answer lies with us, with hearts and minds that support such wreckage, even when we "know better," and the answer lies with laws that will help us change the way we live.

2

GLOBAL WARMING:
A THEOLOGICAL PROBLEM

Jesus must be loved as a world.
— Pierre Teilhard de Chardin[1]

The Time Is Now:
An Analysis of the Problem

In the late 1980s, I attended a meeting of the World Council of
Churches on climate change. I did not know much about it, but the
term sounded relatively benign. I was in for a big surprise. I recall feeling a knot in my stomach when I heard about glacier melt. I wasn't
thinking of the global consequences of submerged islands and coastal
cities. Rather, I was thinking about myself. As a regular hiker in the
Canadian Rockies, I saw the melting of glaciers as a personal loss: I
loved those towering ice-covered mountains circling turquoise lakes.
I felt anger and resentment—not unlike one feels at the unnecessary
death of a friend. How could this awful thing be happening to one of

the most beautiful places on earth? I felt even worse when I was told that *we*, people like myself, were to blame.

Almost twenty years have passed since my introduction to global warming. It has grown, both in my mind and within our culture—after two decades of denial—to epitomize the fragility of the human experiment on earth. We know "the time is now": there is no time left for further denial or delay. Acceptance of the reality of global warming is finally widespread. Denial has been unmasked, although large segments of Western culture have not yet accepted the need for change, and governments and the fuel industry are not eager to take the kind of serious action that is needed. Nonetheless, we are now in a different place than I was twenty years ago: we know that something must be done, and done soon.

Yes, but here's the rub: effective action on global warming is probably the most discouraging task that human beings have ever undertaken. By comparison, mobilizing the Allies in World War II was relatively straightforward. The enemy was clearly identified, and we were the "good guys." Such a war is an in-your-face danger that people react to immediately—and feel good doing so (studies showed that psychological health was up during the war). On the contrary, climate change is slow, insidious, partly invisible—and we are the enemy. Moreover, we are a (largely) innocent enemy: we high-level consumers of energy are merely living ordinary Western lives, doing what everyone else in our society is doing. Even as we gradually learn how deeply our actions are affecting the planet's health, the problem still seems amorphous, abstract, remote. A Katrina hurricane or a torrid summer such as 2003 may jolt us to attention for a while, but the impact fades.

However, let us imagine that a large number of people do become centrally and more or less continually concerned—and *want* to act. The two main avenues for action are personal and political. Many people are attempting to live simpler, more environmentally friendly, low-energy lives by changing behavior at the personal level. But what these folks soon realize is that the corporate and political institutions of our society pose enormous barriers to such personal changes: the lack of low-energy transportation and buildings; a constant barrage of advertisements for SUVs and high-energy electronics and appliances; a global food market that transports produce halfway around the world at an enormous expenditure of energy. Discouragement sets in: Does it make any real difference what individuals do in their personal lives if the culture and political structures are against them?

Let us now imagine that these people decide they must change the systemic structures that are literally "fueling" the energy explosion that is producing global warming. How do they do this? In a democracy, there is only one way: by changing the government—and *that* is possible only by changing people's hearts and minds so that they vote differently. In other words, the political rests on substantial shifts within voting bodies regarding what they want governments to do. Prior to 9/11, a grassroots movement of nongovernmental organizations (NGOs), church groups, and numerous others was beginning to surface, united by the slogan "A different world is possible." Many things were meant by that slogan, but one important thread was certainly an embrace of a communitarian rather than an individualistic view of humanity. At the heart of any revolution bent on changing human behavior lies an anthropology—an understanding of who we human beings are and where we fit into the scheme of things. This communitarian turn is critically important, for it is hard to see how we can tackle our impending climate crisis without it. Sadly, at least for the time being, it is largely dormant, silenced by "the war on terror."

We are, then, in a very difficult place. The kind of thinking we need about ourselves and our place on the planet—our interrelationship and interdependence with all other human beings and other life-forms—has been deadened by the hand of a consumerist/militarist paradigm that exalts the comfort and superiority of elite individual human beings. We *need* to elect representatives to our governments who will create laws to limit human energy use at all levels—from emission caps on oil refineries to regulations on emissions from automobiles. The personal and the political need to join to legislate the kind of human action in the world that will create a just and sustainable planet. Individuals *cannot* do this simply by trying to live "environmentally" within an energy-mad society. The system must be changed—the major forces within society that regulate and control our use of fossil fuels.

I would venture that many of us *want* such regulation. Those who do have a communitarian view of life are asking for help. We cannot live differently—at least with any effectiveness—within a society that allows individuals to use any amount of energy they can afford. We want systemic changes that will help all of us (and all of us like the comforts of a high-energy consumer culture) to live as we ought and want to live. *The time is now*: there is no more time for either denial or delay. We must change our view of ourselves—our anthropology—so that we will elect leaders who can help structure our society in ways that are good not just for some privileged human beings, but for all human beings and all other life-forms. This is what global warming is telling us: we cannot continue to live as selfish individuals, heedless of the consequences of our profligate, adolescent behavior. The ominous tipping point of the global temperature may be less than a few decades away—that point at which gradual global warming tips over into out-of-control exponential heating. Fear is not the reason to change, however, for apocalyptic scenes often come back to haunt us with escapist solutions. Nonetheless, the tipping point stands as a cautionary tale that global warming is not simply "another problem" facing us; in many ways, it epitomizes *the* problem—the problem that starts with our false view of ourselves, the view that we are separate individuals who enter into relationships when we feel like it and who have the right to own all of the worldly goods we can legally get hold of. Increasingly, from all sides—ecology, cosmology, feminist thought, Indigenous Peoples, the NGOs, process theology, and many religions—a common anthropology is emerging: we are not our own; we belong to the earth.

Theology and Anthropology: What Can Religion Tell Us about Ourselves?

Deep down, beneath all of our concepts and ideas about ourselves, is a sense, a feeling, an assumption about who we are. This is not a question people commonly ask of each other—or of themselves—any more than they ask one another, "Who is God?" These questions are seen as too personal or too abstract or too intimidating for civil conversation. Nonetheless, they are the deepest questions of human existence and lie uneasily beneath any glib answers we might give, were we to be asked. However, we act all the time on the basis of these deep assumptions of who we are and who God is, even while not acknowledging that we have such assumptions. When we respond with approval to an advertisement for an expensive, gas-guzzlinng car telling us that "we deserve the very best," we are implicitly acknowledging that privileged individualism is our assumption about human nature. When we say that God is interested in spiritual, not secular, matters (and therefore not in cars), we are implicitly confessing that we believe in a distant, uninvolved God.

Who I am and who God is are taken for granted in a culture: the answer lies with the unacknowledged but accepted conventions of what is meant by "a human being" and "God." But it is precisely the false conventional views of God and ourselves that permit the continuing destruction of our planet and its inhabitants. The environmental crisis is a theological problem, a problem coming from views of God and ourselves that encourages or permits our destructive, unjust actions. For example, if I see myself (deep down) as superior to other animals and life-forms—a privileged individual (Western, white, educated, and so on)—then of course I will act in ways that support my continuation in this position. If, as a human being, I am basically "on my own," then it is also "up to me" to maintain my superiority. This sense of isolated, responsible individualism need not be conscious; in fact, it usually is not. Rather, it is considered by most privileged Western human beings to be simply the way things are. It is seen as "natural" rather than as a personal belief.

Likewise, if I imagine God (deep down) to be a super-being, re-siding somewhere above and apart from the world, who created and judges the world but otherwise is absent from it, then I will conduct my affairs largely without day-to-day concern about God. If the God I believe in is supernatural, transcendent, and only occasionally inter-ested in the world, then this God is not a factor in my daily actions. Whether I treat myself to that high-emissions car is certainly not rel-evant to such a God.

So we are suggesting that *who* God is and *who* we are must be central questions if we hope to change our actions in the direction of just, sustainable planetary living. It is useless to censure people for their actions when the roots of those actions lie in deep, unexamined as-sumptions. The problem lies in our theologies and our anthropologies. The problem, as many have pointed out, is a "spiritual" one, having to do with our *will* to change. We already know more than enough about the disaster ahead of us—having more knowledge (or technology) will not solve the problem. Only changing human wills can do so.

But is this possible? It is not sufficient to "know the good" in order to "do the good." While the Greeks believed this way, the apostle Paul knew better, and most of us think Paul is the better realist. So why bother with new theologies and anthropologies? Aren't they just more "knowledge"? Yes and no. Yes, because obviously they fall into the cat-egory of knowledge, but no, because it is a peculiar kind of knowledge, the deepest possible kind—who we are and who God is. If we change these basic assumptions, our behavior may change as well. To be sure, it will not happen necessarily, easily, or universally, but it can and might happen. Or to put it negatively, unless *another* option becomes available to us, we have nothing to choose but the conventional view of God and ourselves, a view that is destructive of ourselves and our planet.

A Call to Action: Bringing the Church Back Down to Earth

A communitarian view of human beings is an ecological, economic one. It is a view of our place in the scheme of things that sees our well-being as interdependent with all other life-forms in a just, sustainable way. Thus, its basic claims are ecological—we exist only in and with the other living components of our planet—and economic—we must share the planet's resources justly and sustainably if any of us is to flourish.

But most churches today are not "ecological." The Sunday sermon is not about the flourishing of God's whole creation; more often, especially in North American well-off churches, it is aimed at the care and comfort of human individuals. The gospel—the good news—is usually addressed to human needs and failings. Occasionally, on Earth Day and when children help with the service, the environment is brought into the picture. Creation is allowed to take center stage a few times a year. But the well-being of the whole of God's creation is not seen as part and parcel of the gospel message. It is usually an add-on. Christian theology has been anthropocentric—concerned mainly with the well-being of human beings.

But can human beings thrive apart from nature? If salvation is understood as eternal life for some humans, then perhaps the answer is yes. But if salvation means the flourishing of all God's creatures here and now on this earth, then the answer is no. The world cannot be left out. The church must become ecological through and through.

I want to suggest a call to action in three parts. First, I will propose that the church *is* ecological, in a way similar to the classic marks of the church as one, holy, catholic, and apostolic. Second, if the church is ecological, then it (we) must take public stands on issues that affect the well-being of all creation such as global warming. In other words, the church must get involved in economics and do so in ways that advocate

particular public policies. Finally, I offer a two-minute sermon remind-
ing us Christians why we dare to believe that God cares about creation
and works in and through us as we work for its well-being.

The Ecological Church

French theologian Simone Weil wanted to know how Christianity
could call itself catholic if creation was left out.[2] One of the classic
marks of the church—its catholicity or universality—calls for the in-
clusion of *the world*. Another theologian, Pierre Teilhard de Chardin,
puts it this way: "Jesus must be loved as a world."[3] The catholicity of the
church has meant several things over the ages, from "widespread" and
"orthodoxy of belief" to "communion of the saints." However, in spite
of the Oxford English Dictionary's meaning of *catholic*—"as a whole"
or "entire, without exception"—the mark of catholicity when applied
to the church has excluded the world, planet Earth. It has referred only
to human beings: the latent anthropocentrism of Christianity's central
institution, the church, is thus evident in one of its classic marks.

Weil and Teilhard de Chardin suggest a broader definition of *catholic*: it must include the world. God's household is the *whole* planet: it
is composed of human beings living in interdependent relations with
all other life-forms and earth processes. The Greek word for house,
oikos, is the source of our words *ecological, ecumenical,* and *economic.*[4]
If salvation is seen as the flourishing of God's household, then we
must see these three words together. In order for the whole planet to
flourish, the earth's resources must be distributed justly among all its
inhabitants, human and earth others, on a sustainable basis. If salvation means the well-being of all creation—and not just of some human
beings who are saved for life in another world—then the catholicity of
the church demands that "creation not be left out" and that "Jesus be
loved as a world."

This means returning to the oldest and deepest Christian theology: cosmological theology. Theologian George Hendry has suggested
that there are three major contexts for doing Christian theology: the
cosmological, the political, and the psychological.[5] All three are necessary—the integrity of creation, the well-being of all humanity, and
peace for the human spirit. However, during the modern era, the psychological context has predominated: in both evangelical Christianity
and New Age religions, the sin and/or serenity of individuals has been
central. The political context resurfaced in the twentieth century in the

insistence of liberation theologies on the "preferential option for the poor." Finally, ecological theologies have returned Christianity to its roots in the cosmological context. From this context, the redeemer is understood as the creator, whose theater of operation includes all that is. As dwellers of planet Earth, we understand God's household specifically to be our earth. As with Adam and Eve, we have been given this world as the garden to care for. Care for the earth is our primary vocation as God's partners in helping creation to flourish.

The catholicity of the church, understood as its mission to help bring about a just, sustainable planet, has not, however, been the central Christian view for the last several hundred years. Rather, God is imagined as occupying another world while we human beings are sojourners on earth, hoping to return eventually to our true home in heaven. God is seen as spirit, the earth as flesh, and our task is to leave the flesh and attain life in the spirit. This is a strange understanding for an *incarnational* religion. One of the most distinctive characteristics of Christianity is its insistence that God is *with us* in the flesh, here and now, on our earth. Jesus Christ is the paradigm, the explicit good news, that we are not alone on the earth and that we do not belong somewhere else. God is not anti-flesh or anti-world; in fact, just the opposite: the incarnation says that God is the one in whom we live and move and have our being *as* fleshly, earthly creatures. God does not despise the world; God loves the world and expects us to as well.

We have been given permission to love the world by the incarnation of God in the world. Thus, our assignment becomes figuring out what loving the world means. We have been given some hints in the contemporary, evolutionary, ecological worldview of our time that has replaced the three-story universe of heaven, earth, and hell. This new worldview says that all human beings and other life-forms are interrelated and interdependent.[6] We all share the resources of our finite house, planet Earth, and we need each other to survive and flourish. Perhaps most important, this mark of the church—its ecological catholicity—suggests a new interpretation of *who we are in the scheme of things*. In the old picture, human beings were seen as God's darlings, as the special ones who merited salvation in heaven with God. In the new picture, human beings are seen as caretakers of God's household, the earth, just as Adam and Eve were told to tend the garden.

Ecological catholicity is not a minor addition to the marks of the church: it is central to its mission to preach good news to *all* of creation. In many churches today, the gospel preached is principally to needy, anxious human beings seeking a one-on-one relationship with God. Ecological matters are seldom seen as part of the church's central message. That message is only for people, especially people in their personal joys and sorrows. But if Jesus is to be loved *as a world*, if the church is not catholic if the world is left out, then how can we say that such a narrow, individualistic, human-centered gospel is Christian? Do not all three contexts—the cosmological, the political, and the psychological—need to be included since God the redeemer is also the creator of all that is? If we are interdependent and interrelated with all other human beings and life-forms, then the good news must include *all* of us.

This does not mean merely blessing the animals in a service recalling St. Francis, and even less does it mean privileging our pets—the poster animals of the ecological movement. If we are to include the whole earth in the good news, we must become involved in hard economic thinking and decisions. A just, sustainable planet is not possible unless all of its parts have access to resources. The whole cannot be healthy if the parts are sick. In other words, ecological catholicity means the implementation of radical changes in the lifestyle of some parts of the whole—specifically, the 20 percent of human beings who possess 80 percent of the world's resources.[7] This lifestyle, as epitomized in global warming, is making the majority of human beings poor and destroying many other life-forms and earth processes upon which all depend. If ecological catholicity is a mark of the church, if it is—or should be—one of the distinctive characteristics by which the church is known, then Christians, especially well-off ones, *must live differently*. We must live a life of limitation, of "enoughness," indeed, of sacrifice. Discipleship for well-off contemporary Christians means cruciform living: living in solidarity with those who are oppressed and suffering. In our time, such oppression is epitomized by the billion or so human beings who exist on a dollar a day, by other animals that are losing their habitats, and by a deteriorating planet that is dying from our excessive energy use. Thus, *including the world* as a mark of the church is a necessity. Christianity is not a "world religion" if it does not do so. Neither is it faithful to its own gospel: God is with us, all of us, here and now, in our world, on this earth.

The Church and the Public Voice

The privatization of religion is the triumph of public greed. Religion is not intrinsically private—that is, concerned only with God and the soul. Rather, most religions are inexorably public, having to do with some definition of the good life and how to lead it. Christianity is one of these religions that has economics at its heart. You can search the Bible for hours hunting down the few passages on homosexuality (or on sexuality of any sort), while texts on wealth and poverty are everywhere. A case can be made that both the Hebrew scriptures and the New Testament are obsessed with the topic: their motto seems to be Mark 10:25—the rich trying to enter the kingdom of God are like a camel trying to squeeze through the eye of a needle. Why is the Bible so concerned with economics, with money? The answer involves one's definition of salvation.

If salvation means the redemption of individuals from their sins so that they might live eternally in another world, then economics is not a central religious concern. However, if salvation means the well-being of all creation here and now, then economics becomes very important to religion. In fact, both understandings of salvation acknowledge the significance of economics, with the first view fervently denying that money has anything to do with God and the second insisting that it has everything to do with God. The first position says God is only interested in our souls, in spiritual things; the other position claims that God is concerned with the well-being of the whole person, with all persons, and with all other creatures.

The attractiveness of privatizing and spiritualizing salvation is that it leaves us free to collect, hoard, and use for our own benefit all of the goods we can get hold of, while still claiming that we are religious in our personal lives—for instance, by giving generously to charity. The sting of acknowledging salvation to be a matter of public—indeed, of planetary—flourishing is that economics moves to center stage.

I would suggest that if salvation is not merely eternal life for select human beings, but rather as the early theologian Irenaeus puts it—"The glory of God is every creature fully alive"—then the church *necessarily* has a public voice. It is not a choice. To preach the gospel, the church must be involved in public issues of justice and sustainability—in economics. This is so because economics is not just about money; it is about who lives and who dies, and who lives decently and who does not.[8] It is about what is needed for life to flourish. Economics is not only or mainly a specific field of study (like medicine or law). Rather, *economics is the most basic of all human studies*; it is concerned with the laws of our planet: *oikonomia*. It is concerned with good household management. What we see in global warming is a prime example of bad planetary management. *Ecumenical, ecological,* and *economic* all come from the same language root: the three words together provide the rules whereby *all* of us creatures, human and nonhuman, can live sustainably and justly in our house, planet Earth. Planetary economics is the *just* sharing among all of basic, needed resources in a fashion geared to long-term sustainability. Justice and sustainability are the norms that guide the allocation of resources in this model of economics; they are also what is needed to avoid excessive climate change. The central difference between ecological economics and neoclassical economics, the model that rules the global market, is that the first says that for all creatures to have the good life (to be saved), sharing and limitation are necessary, whereas neoclassical economics claims that the good life is reserved for the few who can control the most resources for themselves, with justice and sustainability secondary matters.

Both are economic *models*, that is, visions of the good life. One is not objective, empirical, real, while the other is subjective, normative, utopian. The neoclassical model is based on an assumption, a bias, about who we human beings are: we are basically selfish individuals who, acting out of self-interest, will eventually create some benefits for all in the system. The ecological economic model is also based on an assumption: we are basically interrelated, interdependent creatures who need one another to survive and flourish. In fact, we human beings are the neediest of all creatures, able to last only a few minutes without air, a few days without water, a few weeks without the green plants. If we were to disappear tomorrow, no other creatures would miss us (except our pets), but we cannot live a day without other creatures. The neoclassical economic model is built on a false anthropology: we cannot go it alone.

So why should Christians care about which economic model rules the world? Is there a "Christian" economics? No, I don't think so, but given an understanding of salvation as the flourishing of all creatures— the transformation and fulfillment of creation—then one of these models, I suggest, is closer to the Christian gospel than the other. A case can be made that distributive justice and sustainability, as goals for planetary living, are pale reflections, but reflections nonetheless, of what Jesus meant by the kingdom of God.[9] There are many ways to make this case, but John Dominic Crossan offers a persuasive one in his analysis of the parable of the feast as central to Jesus' understanding of the kingdom.[10] In this story, as you recall, everyone is invited to dinner—the kingdom is known by radical equality at the level of bodily needs. It claims that all are invited to share the food; in other words, *everyone has the right to the basics of existence.* This vision of God's will for the world does not specifically mention just, sustainable planetary living, but throughout the Bible, Scripture is surely more in line with that worldview than with the satisfaction of individual consumer desires.

The eucharistic banquet to which all creatures are invited is, I believe, at the heart of the Christian gospel; it is also faintly reflected in an ecological economic model of planetary living. Within this understanding, especially for us well-off Westerners who own most of the world's resources, sin means the refusal to share, the refusal to work for systemic changes in our laws, institutions, and practices that will help bring about a more just and sustainable planet—a healthy planet able to support life. Thus, global warming is a religious issue. Sin is public and economic; it is not just private and sexual. Christians should, I believe, join with those NGOs claiming that "a different world is possible." We, too, subscribe to this motto and need to work publically and politically to help bring it about.

In sum, neoclassical economics has a vision of the good life. It fits well with privatizing Christianity so that salvation focuses on spiritual matters, the redemption of souls. If Christianity is serious about preaching the gospel in our time, it must enter into public discussion with this vision—both to critique it and to present alternatives to it. This is, I believe, the role of all religions, not just of Christianity. Religions have as much right to argue for their views of the abundant life as do the market forces that endlessly preach a consumer utopia for the privileged few. We, too, must participate in the common planetary agenda that lies before us all.

"Probably the most challenging task facing humanity today is the creation of a shared vision of a sustainable and desirable society, one that can provide permanent prosperity within the biophysical constraints of the real world in a way that is fair and equitable to all of humanity, to other species, and to future generations."[11]

Surely Christians have something to offer to this most challenging task.

But Can We Meet This Challenge?

"For it is the God who said, 'Let light shine out of darkness,' who has shone in our hearts to give the light of the knowledge of the glory of God in the face of Jesus Christ" (2 Cor 4:6). This verse sums up the

Christian story through the image of light: the light that brought creation into being, the light of the glory of God in Jesus Christ, and the light of revelation within us. Creation and salvation in one sentence—and our recognition of both. The same light that created us now saves us *and* shines within us *so that we know it.*

This text is surely one of the most beautiful, heartening, and overwhelming sentences in all of Scripture, because what we now know is the glory of God in the *face* of Jesus Christ. Jesus reveals to us the very heart of God. The one whom we have had in our midst as healer of the sick, liberator of the oppressed, and host to all hungry creatures at the banquet of life—this Jesus, who went to his death for living such a countercultural life—*in his face we see the face of God.* Our creeds tell us that Jesus was of one substance with God, and that is good news, but just as important, we learn that *God is like Jesus*—the mysterious, awesome God of the universe can *be known* in Jesus. Paul is saying that the creator of the universe, the one who "let light shine out of darkness," the God who gives all being and all life, is the same one whom we see in Jesus Christ. And how can we be certain of this? Again, 2 Cor 4:6: the one who let light shine out of darkness has also "shone in our hearts" in order that we may *know*, recognize and acknowledge, that God's glory is in the face of Jesus. In Paul's understanding, God does it all: God creates us, God comes to us in Jesus, and God enlightens us so we recognize God in Jesus.

"For it is the God who said, 'Let light shine out of darkness,' who has shone in our hearts to give the light of the knowledge of the glory of God in the face of Jesus Christ." This is the good news of Christianity. It is overwhelming news. We never could have guessed it on our own. It is, I believe, more astounding, more wonderful than a theology that tells us that Jesus suffered a brutal, gory, violent death for our sins so that God's mind might be changed about us. In Paul's passage, God's mind does not need changing—but our minds do. We *need* to see the glory of God in the face of Jesus and be assured that the God who created us loves us exorbitantly, so exorbitantly that Jesus—the image of God—went to his death in order that the most oppressed, the most marginal, the most despised of us might live. Jesus did not live in order to die; rather, he died in order to live—in order that all of us might see a new way to live. His suffering was in order to open our eyes to the way of the cross, the way in which we all must live so that creation may flourish. The death of Jesus says to us that living in solidarity with others, even when it involves sacrifice and suffering, is the only way to life.

And we know this in the *face* of Jesus Christ. We do not see the glory of God directly, but we meet God in the face of Jesus. We meet God in Jesus eating with outcasts, healing the sick, destabilizing the wealthy and powerful, welcoming the stranger, siding with the oppressed, and inviting everyone to the table. *This* is the glory of God that we see in the face of Jesus: we see that a different world is possible.

PART TWO

Exploring God and
the *World* within
Climate Change

3

WHO ARE WE?
ECOLOGICAL ANTHROPOLOGY[1]

We are not our own. Nothing is itself taken alone. Things are
because of interrelations and interconnections.
— Wallace Stevens[2]

Some Reflections on Individualistic Anthropology

In terms of how we act, probably nothing is more important than who
we *think* we are. Our unconscious or subconscious assumptions concerning our place in the scheme of things lie at the heart of our behavior. Most people are not consciously mean, selfish, or evil; rather, we do
what others in our society do and assume that this is "the way things
are." In Western democratic, capitalist, individualistic societies, the
rights to personal pleasure and gain are taken for granted. While care
for the poor is also a responsibility, such cultures seldom see their role
as justly distributing basic resources so all might live decently. Rather,

the assumption is that individual human beings must take responsibility for themselves, while governments help those who are having difficulty making the grade.

Most people in Western democracies think they are, basically and centrally, "individuals." They do not, first of all, think of themselves as members of a community, not of a human community and even less of a natural or planetary community. This individualistic outlook encourages people to work hard and to compete for scarce resources, and thus to tend to see others—both humans and other life-forms—as resources or objects toward one's goal of self-sufficiency. This model of human life is deeply engrained in our sensibility and functions at every level: in our families, at school, at the office, in sports, and in politics. People are rewarded for individual achievement, without regard to its implications for other people or for nature. Our most basic stance involves standing on our own two feet and viewing others and the world from that vantage point.

But what if this view is false? What if it should turn out that "we are not our own" but belong body and soul to others—other people and other life-forms? What if we discover that individualistic anthropology is a lie, that ecological anthropology is truer to the way things are? What if the consequences of climate change are telling us that we are living in ways that our planet will not allow? What if we begin to realize that the community model—the model in which human individuals must fit into a just, sustainable planet—is a necessity? What if we wake up from our dream of individualistic glory, regardless of the consequences to others, and realize that either we will all make it together, or none of us will make it? What if a very different view of who we *think* we are should become common, become conventional, become "natural"?

This concept is emerging as a possibility from many places, and its growth worldwide may be central to our ability to respond to the crisis of our time—global warming. Global warming is not just another important issue that human beings need to deal with; rather, it is the demand that we *live differently*. We cannot solve it, deal with it, given our current anthropology. It is not simply an issue of management; rather, it demands a paradigm shift in *who we think we are*. This is certainly not the only thing that is needed, but it is a central one, for without it we cannot expect ourselves or others to undertake the radical behavioral change that is necessary to address our planetary crisis. Hence, what follows is a primer in ecological anthropology.

Why Ecological Anthropology?

When I was a theology student in the 1950s, describing anthropology as "ecological" would have made no sense. Anthropology was about human beings, period. Indeed, the focus of the Christian study of humanity was radically anthropocentric, centered on human beings (not in relation to nature or creation), and more specifically, on human beings as *individuals before God*. Isn't Christian theology about people being saved? What does it have to do with the environment? Since the Protestant Reformation, the focus of Christian theology had narrowed from its original scope, including all of creation, to a pinpoint: the self with God. The turn to the subject, to the individual human being, which began with Protestantism's concern with individuals and their relationship with God, reached its culmination in twentieth-century existentialism. With science taking over nature, theology retreated to the inner life of individuals in their alienation from God and struggle to believe in God. It was a narrow field of operation, and one in which "ecological anthropology" would make no sense. Christian faith was proudly claimed to be a historical, not a nature, religion: concerned with man's (*sic*) "spirit," not his body. Nature religions were implicitly considered inferior to those focused on human beings and their eternal fate. Implicit also in this picture is the conventional assumption that human beings are superior to other creatures: the Genesis command to subdue and dominate, while not necessarily encouraged, was seldom refuted. Theology simply didn't pay much attention to nature, creation, or other life-forms, nor to human beings in their relationships with these realities. Human beings were understood to be *individuals in relation to God*, either properly or improperly related. The contemporary heirs of existentialist individualism—born-again Christians as well as some New Age adherents—carry on the focus on individual human beings with concern for the salvation and/or therapy of individuals.

This theological focus on the individual meshed well with the anthropology emerging from two other American institutions—economics and government. The economic man (*sic*) of market capitalism is the insatiable individual whose desire for endless consumer goods fuels the system and is necessary for this economic model to function. Likewise, since the eighteenth century and the founding documents of American government, the "life, liberty, and pursuit of happiness" of individuals have comprised the signature statement of American anthropology.

When the three major societal institutions of religion, economics, and government all agree on a basic anthropology—one that focuses on, supports, and celebrates the needs and wants of individuals—a powerful statement is being made. These institutions are implicitly forming the unconscious and semiconscious assumptions of citizens in regard to what they can and should do in their personal, professional, and public lives. These pillars of society—religion, economics, and government—spread a canopy over "individualism," blessing it while at the same time creating a formidable barrier against alternative anthropologies. The witch hunts of the 1950s in the United States to ferret out Communist anthropology (a communitarian perspective) illustrate the point. The individualistic paradigm of human life pretends to be the truth, the way things are, rather than an interpretation, a model, a possibility of how we should live.

Are We the Only Ones Who Matter?

Contemporary science suggests a different picture of who we are in the scheme of things than is found in the North American consensus. In fact, it is radically different. Rather than starting with human individuals—their needs or wants—the scientific view begins with the cosmic story of the evolution of the universe. Some fifteen billion years ago, a tiny bit of matter imploded—the Big Bang—resulting in the billions of galaxies in the universe, as well as our tiny planet Earth, and the life that eventually appeared on it. This story, which is now universally accepted among scientists publishing in peer-reviewed journals, is the necessary beginning point for any twenty-first-century anthropology. It is a cosmological, evolutionary, ecological story; that is, it includes everything that is; it claims everything has evolved from that tiny exploding bit of matter billions of years ago; and it implies, therefore, that all things are interrelated and interdependent in both macro and micro ways. It is a story that begins with radical unity evolving into unimaginable diversity, but diversity that is intrinsically and internally interconnected. It is a story in which we human beings are, at present, the most complex developed creatures on earth, yet we are imbedded in, the products of, the earth and its evolution. We share a common origin with everything else: the same biochemical elements are in bacteria and in us. Most recently, we have learned that we share a good deal of our DNA with mice, not to mention the 98 percent we share with our closest relatives, chimpanzees. When viewed in the womb, the early stage development of embryos—frog, chicken, and human being—is very similar. We, as the most complex life-form on earth, could not have arrived any earlier than we did: we needed the billions of years of the evolving universe for us to appear. We are part and parcel of all that has gone before us: they are our ancestors, our kin, our roots.

And yet we are special, as is everything else. Our "specialty" is self-consciousness: we know that we know. All sentient creatures know many things—how to find food, ward off predators, raise off-spring—but human beings appear to be the only ones who can *think about* what we know (at least in the highly developed way we do). We know that we were born and that we will die: we have created stories, music, dances, paintings, philosophies, and religions, as well as mind-altering substances to help us deal with this awesome knowledge. As the symbol-making creatures par excellence, we have the peculiar, painful, and wonderful distinction of knowing that we know.

We are by no means the only distinctive creatures: all creatures are. Would a dolphin think we could swim? An eagle that we could fly? A deer that we could run? We are certainly not the "measure" of other creatures, as people once thought who graded other life-forms in terms of their closeness to or distance from our peculiar form of "reason." That false anthropocentrism has been left behind as we have come to appreciate our particular role not as the measure of all things, but as the measurer—the ones who can admire, reflect on, take care of all the rest. What our peculiar distinction has led us to see is that, given our present numbers and power, we have the ability to be either for or against the rest of nature. We are not the only ones who matter, but we are the ones who are increasingly responsible for the others in creation.

We have arrived at this knowledge at the same time that we realize that we are not separate, static individuals who choose to be in relations with other life-forms when we feel like it. Rather, we now know that we belong, from the cells of our bodies to the finest creations of our minds, to the intricate, changing cosmos that gave us birth and sustains us. "We are not our own," as Wallace Stevens puts it. "Nothing is itself taken alone. Things are because of interrelations and interconnections."[3] It is this combination of responsibility and interdependence that is the key to contemporary, scientific anthropology. We are responsible, we can make choices, we can decide to live one way or another, but we are not just responsible for our individual selves. Rather, we now know that "who we are" is interconnected with all other living things. We evolved together with the cosmos, and we are entirely dependent on certain conditions on planet Earth (water, food, land, climate, and so on) for our continued existence and well-being. Suddenly we see ourselves differently: not as post-Enlightenment individuals who have the right to life, liberty, and the pursuit of happiness, but as part of a vast network of interrelationships, and specifically as that "part" responsible for the rest, for other human beings and other life-forms. Western societies have spent the last three hundred years internalizing an anthropology of radical individualism; we now must internalize a profoundly different anthropology if our planet is to survive and flourish. While it is difficult to imagine, let alone internalize—and live—this new anthropology, nowhere is it more evident that we must do so than with the issue of climate change.

Climate is the broadest, deepest, most intricate system on earth. It controls everything else: water, land, the sun, food. It makes some places desirable, other places undesirable; some places habitable, other places inhabitable. The quality of the "space" for humans and other life-forms depends on climate. What global warming is illustrating with brutal realism is how vulnerable living creatures are to even a few degrees' change in the earth's average temperature. Regardless of where one lives on the earth, and regardless of one's status, everyone and everything will be affected, for climate is the quintessential example of interrelationship and interdependence. It may well be that the threat of global warming will be the opening for Westerners to begin to see themselves differently: not as self-sufficient individuals who can barricade themselves safely in gated communities, but as creatures dependent on a temperate global climate, as are all living things. It is not easy to change one's picture of who we are in the scheme of things. We need a wake-up call, and it is hard to imagine a more clarion one than global warming. The picture we see before us contains the sickening sight of skinny polar bears balancing on receding ice floes and children dying of thirst in a parched desert.

Ecological Literacy

The study of ecology is the most basic knowledge that we need to help us make the shift to a new way of seeing ourselves. Ecology is, at its simplest, "words about home": *oikos* (home) and *logos* (word). Ecology is not an esoteric subject reserved for experts, but information about planet Earth—its nature and its rules, and hence where we fit into it. Ecology is a study that should begin in infancy and continue through adulthood. If we are to turn away from anthropocentrism—the focus on ourselves as masters of the earth—to cosmocentrism—the focus on the earth and where we belong in it—we need a *functional* creation story. We need a story about ourselves and our earth that will *work*: that is, a story that will help all of us live justly and sustainably in our home, planet Earth. The sciences are providing us with such a story, and, interestingly, it fits well with the oldest and deepest Christian creation story. This theological story also asks us to broaden our perspective from "the soul and God" to the whole earth: in Christian faith, the redeemer is also the creator. Hence, ecological theology is not a New Age fad; rather, it returns this tradition to its cosmological roots. God is God of *all* creatures. We are not the only ones who matter: God cares for the sparrow and the lilies. This refocusing of knowledge, both secular and theological, to an ecological context is not sentimental nature worship. Rather, it is a recognition of the three contexts in which Christian theology has been and should be done.[4] They are the cosmological, the political, and the psychological: the earth as a whole, the world of human oppression, and the inner life of the individual. Each of these contexts is important and should be included in all Christian theologies. They form a whole, a set of concentric circles, with the cosmological the deepest and widest, serving as the context for the other two—historical oppression and individual fulfillment. Since the Protestant Reformation and the Enlightenment, the focus of Christian theology has moved toward the psychological circle, with increasing marginalization of the political and the cosmological. We have seen a similar movement in secular thought during this period, until the cult of individualism has overtaken our sense of responsibility for the care of creation, as well as our obligations toward other people, especially oppressed or poor people. To widen our perspective, to embrace the earth and all others, is to return to a more fundamental and functional anthropology: one that sees human life embedded in and dependent on the world in which we live. The "turn to the self" of the last few hundred years is an anomaly in human history: prior to that time, and still for many native peoples, we imagined ourselves as *within* nature, not above or apart from it.

Hence, "ecological literacy" is not some newfangled secret knowledge. It simply reminds us of where we came from and where we belong: from nature and in nature. Both Christian theology and contemporary science are telling us that we must *start with the world* in order to understand ourselves: who we are and where we belong. Such a beginning point may help to dampen our astounding egocentrism, evident in our ruthless laying waste of our planet and its other inhabitants, as well as our consigning many of our own species to poverty. A brief rehearsal of our egocentrism against this new creation story tells us that on the universe's time clock, human beings appeared only a fraction of a second before midnight; that we humans need the other inhabitants of the planet much more than they need us—as the creature at the top of the food chain, we are dispensable, whereas the plants and microorganisms in the ocean are essential; and that since we are at present the planet's most dangerous force, all other species would be better off without us. From our former status as the "apex of evolution" and the "darlings of creation," we have become the rogue elephant, rampaging across our planet in reckless fashion.

So what does ecology have to do with this problem? Ecology is not a hobby; it is not an activity for Sierra Club types; it is not a pastime (some folks like hockey while others enjoy bird-watching). Ecology is the most fundamental study imaginable. It is information about how our house works: it is our "house rules." Ecology is the study of earth's organisms along with everything that affects them; it is the study of organisms in their homes and their interactions with one another. Once this basic knowledge is learned, it is difficult to deny. Once we learn, for instance, of the impact of human-generated greenhouse gases on the planet and its creatures, we have difficulty seeing global warming as a myth perpetrated by "eco-radicals."

The most important and simplest house rule is also the most complex and difficult to internalize: *everything is related to everything else*. It is one of those platitudes that says it all but takes a lifetime to understand—rather like another one: God is love. For Christians, those three words sum up the entire faith; everything we say about God, the world, ourselves, our hopes and our commitments, our joys and our sufferings, is implicit in that statement. All interpretations of the major Christian doctrines are variations of that phrase. We hear it as children and when we are on our deathbeds: on the journey between these two points, we hope to gain a sense of what it really means, how we can internalize God's love into every moment of our lives, the wonderful and the despairing moments, as well as the ordinary ones.

A similar task awaits us with "everything is related to everything else." This task is especially challenging for us North American individualists, whose sensibility has been formed in exactly the opposite fashion. We marvel when we hear that pesticides used on roses in Kansas City affect lions in the African veldt, or that deforestation in the Amazon basin influences the survival of algae in a lake in Manitoba. We think of these events as separate—like atoms—when in reality, the more accurate analogy is fishes in the ocean or a baby in the womb.

A personal example may help. In the spring of 1986, during the Chernobyl nuclear incident, my son was on a school trip to Moscow. I, on sabbatical leave in England, had flown to the Greek islands for a vacation. Of course, I was anxious about the radiation my son might be exposed to. However, because of the wind pattern, the radiation missed Moscow, went over the Scandinavian countries, and ended up in England—where I would have been, had I not decided to take a trip. There is no "safe place" on earth where pollution, global warming, acid rain, and so on can't find us—and the places we think are safe can turn out to be the most dangerous.

Buddhist Thich Nhat Hanh has a fine description of our phrase "everything is related to everything else":

> When we look at a chair, we see the wood, but we fail to observe the tree, the forest, the carpenter, or our own mind. When we meditate on it, we can see the entire universe in all its interwoven and interdependent relations in the chair. The presence of the wood reveals the presence of the tree. The presence of the leaf reveals the presence of the sun. The presence of the apple blossoms reveals the presence of the apple. Meditators can see the one in the many and the many in the one. . . . The chair is not separate. It exists only in its interdependent relations with everything in the universe. It *is* because all other things *are.*[5]

Another way to help internalize our phrase—everything is related to everything else—is to recall the classic problem of "the one and the many," or how things can be united into a whole and at the same time be distinct and different. Since the time of Plato, the tendency in the West has been to solve this problem by compromising the many for their unity in the one. An example of this is the metaphor in the United States of the melting pot: people of different nationalities and ethnic backgrounds are "stirred" into the pot and emerge as the prototypical

American. Diversity is sacrificed for the sake of conformity to an ideal type. The Canadian metaphor of the mosaic allows for different groups of people to occupy separate places in the country's self-image, but with a lessened sense of common identity. However, the metaphor of ecological unity solves the problem of the one and the many: the whole is nothing but each of the parts doing its own thing, while the particular parts depend for their existence on the whole. For example, a healthy old-growth forest is composed of many different species and millions of different individual plants and animals, all working together to form the whole. The forest does not exist apart from the myriad life-forms that constitute it, while the individuals depend totally on the whole. Here we have a metaphor, ecological unity, that supports radical unity *and* radical individuality—neither the one nor the many exists without the other—while at the same time underscoring the deepest understanding of both unity and individuality.

It is immediately evident what such a view of the one and the many might do when applied to world peace and planetary flourishing. If this understanding became widespread, became the working assumption of our political and economic institutions, a quiet revolution might take place. Politicians and economists would acknowledge that the whole—nation or planet—could not flourish apart from the health of the parts, both human beings and other creatures. Unfortunately, we are still often operating with the faulty metaphors of the melting pot and the mosaic, which privilege either the whole or the parts at the expense of the other.

"Everything is related to everything else" begins to take on flesh and substance. We can begin to see why it is a way of thinking about ourselves and our world that is a repudiation of both totalitarianism (the rule of the one) and libertarianism (the rule of individuals). It makes a claim about "reality," about the way things are, and admonishes us that if it is the case that all things exist because of their interrelationships and interdependence with one another, then we had best structure our personal, economic, and political lives on this paradigm. Of course, this is an *interpretation* of reality, not a description of it (there are no descriptions). But given what contemporary science is telling us about ourselves and our world, ecological unity is closer to the way things are than is the melting pot or the mosaic. Since we only have interpretations, not descriptions, we must make a judgment as to which interpretation, which metaphor, is the one on which we should base our thoughts and our actions.

If we were to accept ecological unity as the working interpretation for our dealings with each other and with our world, we would have two responses: *appreciation* and *care*. We would see ourselves as part of the web of life, an incredibly vast, complex, subtle, beautiful web that would both amaze us and call forth our concern. We would feel awe about and care for our planet. It would be similar to the difference between imagining the world as a hotel and imagining it is a home. The Western practice has certainly been closer to hotel than home. In a hotel, the utilitarian perspective dominates: one uses hot water copiously, orders from the room service menu whatever one wishes, dumps the thick, dirty towels on the floor, and heads down the road to the next night's hotel. The world as hotel is a resource, solely for human use, including excessive use, if one so desires. This attitude toward the world could be called the "Kleenex® perspective": use and discard. If, however, the earth were to be seen as our home, our one and only home, our response to it is likely to be very different. One appreciates a home and wants to care for it. The very word *home* has deep resonances for most people; it is where one belongs, where one feels "at home." The home metaphor immediately brings to mind the necessity for house rules, the kind one pins on the refrigerator for all occupants to see and obey. They are usually something like the following: (1) Take only your share. (2) Clean up after yourself. (3) Keep the house in good repair for others. Simple to understand, but immensely difficult to live out when we consider them in relation to the earth as our home, our house.

The *oikos* base of ecology is also the base for economics and ecumenicity. In other words, "ecological literacy," words about our house, are at the same time words about economics and about the whole earth. In its simplest formulation, ecological literacy is the words (laws) of economics that we need to learn so that *all* inhabitants of the house, our earth, can live together justly and sustainably. Ecology and economics are obvious partners, for if ecology is the study of earth's organisms along with everything that affects them, then the just sharing of resources is the necessary basis for all to flourish. Ecology is not, then, a pastime for people who enjoy watching birds or identifying different tree species. Rather, it is about life and death, about which animals and plants have the means (air, water, food, habitat, and so on) to flourish—and which do not. Ecological literacy is *basic* survival knowledge.

Let us, then, expand on a few of the most important house rules, beyond the first rule that says everything is related to everything else.

How does the earth work? What are its most fundamental laws? *All processes, both animate and inanimate, occur through energy exchanges.* Energy is involved whenever work is done, when anything speeds up or slows down, is heated or cooled, moves or changes, and so on. The rules of how energy works are known as the first and second laws of thermodynamics, and they are the most basic laws governing our home. The first law is relatively benign; it says that while energy can be converted from one form to another, it is neither created nor destroyed. For example, fossil fuels can be converted into heat or electricity converted into motion. Here only the form has changed, not the quantity. However, the second law presents the problem, for while the quantity remains the same, the quality decreases, tending toward randomness or disorder (entropy). For example, fossil fuels cannot be recycled back into gas or coal but are dissipated into the atmosphere as carbon dioxide. This is the bad news: not only is the new form less usable, but it also can be injurious (as in global warming from greenhouse gases).

These laws govern the living and the nonliving. Thus, as living things seem to increase in order, they always do so by causing a decrease somewhere else, by sucking orderliness from their environment. A good example is the high level of orderliness in cites versus the price paid for this comfort and complexity by "nature"—clear-cutting forests, degrading arable land, lowering diversity in fisheries, draining water from aquifers, and so on. City life is high-energy life: millions, billions, of transformations of energy must occur every hour for us North Americans to live as we wish and as we have become accustomed to living. With every energy exchange—from the ones moving our cars to those powering our electric toothbrushes—a decrease occurs, quality is lost, something somewhere "pays." There is no free lunch.

The second law says we live on a finite planet, and our energy sources are running out. In order for the world's population to live the comfortable, orderly lives that the top fifth of us enjoy, several more planets would be necessary. We are spending down the capital, so to speak; or in house rule language, if we keep raiding the fridge this way, there will be nothing left to eat.

But what about the sun? Is that not our hope, the endless source of energy beyond our finite planet? It is certainly the source of all energy, both renewable and nonrenewable energy. But there is also a cautionary note, which we can see when we consider the three types of living things and where we human beings fit into the scheme. The first type are the "producers," the self-feeders, such as plants that convert the sun's energy through photosynthesis into carbohydrates. The plants and the microorganisms in the ocean are the foundation of the food chain, and all the rest of us depend on them. The second type of living things are the "consumers": *all* of us fit into this category. Every living creature from the microscopic to elephants—including human beings—are consumers. One must consume in order to live. The third type are the "decomposers," the bacteria and fungi that release molecules to be recycled.

The important feature in this analysis of the types is where *we* fit: all we do is consume. We neither produce nor decompose (albeit we eventually and reluctantly contribute our bodies for decomposition!). As consumers, only consumers, and increasingly the largest, most insatiable, and most selfish consumers the planet has ever known, we are becoming a great danger. Our twenty-first-century culture is known as the "consumer culture," and we are identified in our society principally as consumers (rather than as parents, workers, citizens, and so on). Given our highly vulnerable position in this food chain, we would be wise to proceed with caution, but in fact we are doing exactly the opposite. As our numbers increase, so do our "wants" as well as our inability to distinguish them from "needs."

The second law brings us up short. It reminds us of "limits" (a word so alien to consumer culture): that every transformation decreases available energy; that plants cannot thrive when soil and water are degraded; that climate change can alter the energy sources available to human beings; that excessive population plus an excessive lifestyle is a formula for disaster. With a shock of recognition, we realize that we have not been obeying the house rules. We do indeed think there is a free lunch. We do not admit that every energy exchange costs. We do not, for instance, figure in environmental degradation when we price goods: lumber costs do not include the services provided by a forest that is clear-cut—air conditioning, control of soil erosion, medicinal biodiversity, recreation, and so on. These essential services that nature gives us, ranging from climate control to hikes in the woods, are considered "externalities" by market economics and therefore "without value." They are not factored into the price of products. This shocking practice is one of the clearest examples of our outrageous behavior as "housemates"—by this practice, we show that we do not deserve to live in this bountiful house.

Would we behave differently if we saw ourselves differently—as genuine housemates? That is the assumption of this book—that we might. Anthropology is the key doctrine for our own survival and flourishing, as well as those of our planet.

The Consequences of Ecological Illiteracy

But what if we refuse to become ecologically literate? What if we continue to think of ourselves as superior to and independent of the rest of the planet? If we continue to think in this fashion, it is unlikely that our behavior will change. Seeing ourselves differently is the first and perhaps necessary step toward changing behavior. It is certainly no guarantee of behavior change, but it at least gives us a chance, a *choice*, to behave differently. One of the most important forces behind behavior change is the belief that things *can* be different, that what we do makes a difference. A common motto of many NGOs—"A different world is possible"—rests on this belief in the human ability to imagine alternative worlds and to work for their realization.

We must begin to see ourselves as interrelated and interdependent with the animate and inanimate elements of our planet and begin to follow earth's house rules of limited use, recycling, and long-term sustainability. These house rules now take on new depth.

Take only your share. Since all creatures must have food in order to survive, distributive justice becomes a necessary and central human behavior. The whole, the planet, cannot flourish unless the parts are healthy. Hence, "Take only your share" is not a plea for charity to the disadvantaged; rather, it is a law of planetary well-being.

Clean up after yourself. We live in a home, not a hotel, and this home is the only one we will ever have. We must reuse, not use up, everything on the planet. In a healthy ecosystem, everything is recycled: we need to structure our societies on that model. This will not be easy, for our consumer culture thrives on its exact opposite—throwing away.

Keep the house in good repair for others. The house is not ours; we do not own it. Rather, it is on loan to us for our lifetime, and we must sustain it for others.

These house rules, which are relatively easy to understand at a personal level, become much more complex when applied regionally, nationally, and globally. For instance, what is one's "share," or the "share" of a developed country versus that of a developing one, or the "share" of human beings versus that of other life-forms (as in the old debate between loggers' salaries and the survival of the spotted owl)? "Take only your share" is a rough guide—initially meaning no more perhaps than its opposite, "Take all you can get." Figuring out what is a fair share of vital resources for all needy creatures, both human and nonhuman, is an enormous task. It is a task that will involve not only the moral will of all of us, but also the expertise of many discrete fields of study, including economics, agriculture, hydrology, medicine, law, and many others. The reason, however, for optimism in regard to this massive task is that human beings have proven many times, especially in times of war, that they are capable of undertaking enormously complex enterprises, if the will to do so is strong.

The magnificence and bounty of planet Earth are a marvel for our delight and our nourishment; this world is not our possession to be squandered and destroyed. The long-term sustainability of the earth is our goal. This cannot be attained unless we fit our little economy into the planet's big economy. We must live with limits, with justice, with the long view. This need not be a call for asceticism, for anxiety, or for despair. Rather, it is a new vision of the abundant life, not one in which a few live like kings while the rest exist as slaves, and not one in which human desires destroy other life-forms. Rather, it is a vision of just, sustainable abundance.

But we have been living very differently. Our population, and especially the lifestyle that most people desire, is diametrically opposed to this vision. We human beings now control most of the earth's food, water, and space at the price of other animals and plants diminishing and going extinct. Usually, the exponential growth of a species is controlled by limited resources, but our species, and especially the elite 20 percent of us, have figured out how to control and hoard most of the food, water, and space for ourselves. However, unlimited population growth combined with a high-energy lifestyle pushes the animate and inanimate energy sources of our planet to the limit. *We cannot live without these "others."* They are not just the resources for our desires; they are the sources of our existence. This is why a functional creation or cosmology is so important, for we need an appropriate understanding of who we are in the scheme of things. We need to acknowledge our place as dependent and interrelated with all other life-forms in order to attain a just, sustainable planet where we—and the others—can flourish. Even the most anthropocentric anthropology—a view that sees our well-being as all that matters—cannot attain its goal if the planet is not also well and healthy. We cannot go it alone! We cannot do so, *even if we want to.*

All theology is contextual: there is no theology "in general." It always presupposes a context, a place, in which one stands to speak about who we human beings are. Thus, our theological anthropologies speak from the contexts of race, class, gender, sexual orientation, physical ability, geographical location, and so on. But there is one context that has been neglected in the last few hundred years: human beings as a species among many others living in a home we all share. Thus, several decades ago, the World Council of Churches enlarged its motto from "Peace and justice" to "Peace, justice, and the integrity of creation." Peace and justice *depend* on a healthy ecosystem, for there can be no peace or justice unless the basics of existence are available to all. Hence, in addition to the many other contexts for interpreting who we are, we also must remember the cosmological one. We must move beyond democracy to biocracy, beyond loyalty to our own tribe to a view of ourselves as citizens of planet Earth.

So why should theology be concerned with "ecological literacy"? Why should it trouble itself with such mundane things as plants, the second law, population, energy use, and so on? If "salvation" means the well-being of all God's creatures—and not just eternal life in another world for a few chosen human beings—then issues such as climate change, food, energy, the consumer lifestyle, economics, and forest and water management become *theological* issues. A theological anthropology must therefore be rooted in reality, in the way our earth functions, in the details of what makes for earthly flourishing.

We can see now that ecological anthropology is neither an esoteric knowledge for specialists nor a sentimental plea to "love nature." Rather, it is *the truth about who we are*—the best truth, at least, that we presently have. It tells us where we fit in the scheme of things. It is a cautionary tale in light of the way we have been living. It claims that our pretension to being the center of the planet, rather than one of its neediest creatures, is false. It tells us that we have been *living a lie.* It reminds us that instead of being the center of creation, we are from moment to moment dependent on all that is, so to speak, "beneath us" (all of the animate and inanimate energy sources). They are our lifeblood. This new picture of ourselves is especially at odds with those who suppose that "according to Genesis" human beings are to subdue and dominate all others. This picture reminds us that we have been decentered as God's darlings, and recentered as God's partners, the ones who can help work for a just and sustainable planet.

We can see now, perhaps, how radically this ecological context changes how we think about ourselves. Instead of the only ones who matter, we have become the caretakers of everything else. Thomas Berry claims that we have been acting like brash adolescents out of control, as seen in Western individualism, consumerism, and militarism.[6] Once we realize that we are neither the owners nor the principal tenants of our planet, but rather its "adults"—the species that knows the common creation story—we can become God's helpers to see it continue and prosper.

4

WHO IS GOD?
CREATION and PROVIDENCE

We wake, if we wake at all, to mystery, rumors of death, beauty, violence. . . . "Seem like we're just set down here," a woman said to me recently, "and don't nobody know why." . . . Some unwonted, taught pride diverts us from our original intent, which is to explore the neighborhood, view the landscape, to discover where it is that we have been so startlingly set down, even if we can't learn why.
—Annie Dillard, Pilgrim at Tinker Creek[1]

Climate Change and the Question of God

When we wake up to the mystery that surrounds us, its beauty and its violence, we ask, *why* are we here? "Seem like we're just set down here, and don't nobody know why." Indeed. Most religions are about suggesting answers to that question, which is a fiendishly difficult one.

A somewhat easier, more immediate question is the other one: Where are we? As Annie Dillard suggests, "our original intent," as witnessed by a child's interest in and wonder at all things, is "to explore the neighborhood, . . . to discover *where* it is that we have been so startlingly set down, even if we can't learn why."

Climate change demands that we turn our eyes to the world, to space and place, to the concrete; it demands that we ask questions about how to live within the particularities and limitations of planet Earth rather than speculating about why we are here. Instead of focusing mainly on the why questions, should religions give greater attention to learning where we are, what the world is like, and where we fit into it? For instance, on the matter of creation and providence, is it a question of why, when, and how the world was created that is critical, or is it rather discovering the nature, potential, and limitations of our neighborhood, where we live? Is talk about creation and providence concerned with intellectual questions of *why* things are the way they are, or is it about *how* we should live in harmony with all the rest of creation? Christianity has traditionally been focused on the why questions rather than turning our eyes to the beauty, concrete details, processes, and uniqueness of our home, planet Earth. In Christian theology, creation and providence often have been more about God and God's power—evidence that God is in charge—than about human beings living in and caring for the neighborhoods in which we have been set down. The why and where questions are of course interlinked—we will always wonder about the mystery of why we are where we are—but it may be necessary, given climate change, for Christian theology to pay more attention to the wonderful, fragile, complex—not to mention breathtakingly beautiful and violent—world that we actually inhabit. If creation and providence are not just about God creating and caring for the world but also about us living in it and helping it flourish, then creation and providence are about the *most basic* relationship between God and the world. How distant, how close, are God and the world? Is God only transcendent over the world or also immanent in it? Is the relationship between God and the world more like that between a potter and a bowl or like that between a mother and a child? Are we only externally related to God, or are we internally related? Is the world more like another "subject" to God or more like an "object"? Is God "spirit" while the world is only "matter"? Does God have all power over creation, or are human beings also responsible for creation? Are we puppets or partners? These and many more questions dealing with the *nature* of the relationship between God and the world lie at the heart of different interpretations of creation and providence.

I will suggest that the traditional creation-providence story in Christian history has underscored God's power over divine love, God's transcendence over divine immanence, God's distance from the world over God's involvement in it. This need not, should not, be the case: interpreting the God-world relationship based on the belief that *God is incarnate in the world* implies rethinking the issues of creation and providence in light of the world as internally related to God— the world as within God or the world as God's "body"—rather than externally related as an artist is to his or her production. The thesis is, then, that the doctrines of creation and providence are implications drawn from our most basic belief about the God-world relationship, and for Christians this relationship is incarnational: God is with us, here and now, in this world. Our doctrines of creation and providence do not stand alone: they are offshoots of our deepest beliefs about the nature of God's relation to the world. If we believe God and the world are wholly other, we will see creation and providence in that light; if we believe God and the world are intrinsically intimate, we will understand creation and providence from within that perspective. An incarnational context for understanding the God-world relationship has implications for our response to climate change. It means that *we and God are in the same place and that we share responsibility for the world.*

We will unfold this thesis first by looking at the traditional creation myth; then by examining a range of models of the God-world relationship that have functioned in Christian history; and finally by fleshing out what we mean by an incarnational understanding of creation and providence. We will approach the issues of creation and providence in light of basic models of the God-world relationship, focusing our interest not primarily on why, when, and how God created the world, but on the implications of each model for the well-being of all creation and the ways in which human beings can be part of that flourishing. We will focus not on the why, but on the where: How can we all live justly and sustainably in the neighborhoods in which we have so startlingly been set down?

The Traditional Creation Myth

The First Vatican Council (1890) expresses the God-world relationship that, with some variations, is a common one in major creeds of various Christian churches since the Reformation and lies behind the traditional creation-providence story.

> The Holy, Catholic, Apostolic, Roman Church believes and confesses that there is one true and living God, Creator and Lord of Heaven and earth, almighty, eternal, immense, incomprehensible, infinite in intelligence, in will, and in all perfection, who, although He is one, singular, altogether simple and unchangeable spiritual substance, must be pure and distinct in reality and essence from the world, most Blessed in Himself and of Himself, and ineffably most high above all things which are or can be conceived outside Himself.[2]

Given this view of the God-world relationship—one of total distance and difference—the story of creation and providence follows. That story, in its simplest form, claims that an absolute, all-powerful, transcendent God created the world (universe) from nothing for entirely gratuitous reasons. God did not need creation, nor is God internally related to it: it was created solely for God's glory. Unfortunately, creation "fell" through the pride of one of its creatures—human beings—making it necessary for God to initiate a reversal of creation's downfall through Jesus Christ, who atones for the sins of all human beings. In this story, creation and providence are part of one coherent, historical, all-inclusive drama in which *God is in charge* from beginning to end, creating all things and saving them through the atoning blood of his own Son.

This mythic story focuses on God's actions—God is the protagonist of the world drama—and its purpose is to answer why, not where, questions. The story speaks to our concerns about why the world was made, who is in charge of it, why it is no longer harmonious, and how it is made "right" again. This story does not speak to our interest in the world or how we should act toward our neighbors. Human beings are, in fact, minor players in the classic Christian story of creation and providence. Moreover, the action does not occur in our physical neighborhoods, the actual spaces and places we inhabit, but over our heads, as it were, in the vast panoramic historical sweep of time, with its beginning (creation), middle (redemption), and end (eschatology). In each of these events, God is totally in charge; we, at most, like good children are grateful to our almighty, all-loving Father and try to follow his will. Even when sin and evil divert the drama from its triumphant course (and cause us to lose faith and hope), the Lord of history will prevail; the King will be victorious.

What is left out of this story of creation is creation itself, that is, the "neighborhood," the lowly, concrete, particular—and fascinating, wonderful—details of physical reality. It is about history, not geography: about God's action through the sweep of time, not about our life on planet Earth. In fact, the story does not seem to be *about* creation, but about a God who "must be pure and distinct in reality and essence from the world."[3] This God does not inhabit creation; in fact, the assumption behind this creation story is that spirit and matter are entirely distinct and in a dualistic, hierarchical relationship. God and all things spiritual, heavenly, and eternal are perfect and exalted above all things material, earthly, and mortal, with the latter being entirely different from the former and inferior to it. It is difficult to overstate the importance of this assumption—the dualistic, hierarchical relationship of God and the world—for it not only encourages an understanding of salvation as the escape of individuals to the spiritual world, but also justifies lack of attention to the flourishing of this world. If God is spirit and creation is matter, then God does not occupy the earth and we need not attend to it either. But what if spirit and matter were not entirely different; what if all life—God's and ours, as well as that of all others on earth—was seen to be on a continuum, more like a circle or the recycle symbol than like a dualistic hierarchy? What if spirit and matter were intrinsically related rather than diametrically opposed? Would not this make a difference in how we think of *where God is* and *where we should be?* Would it not turn our eyes to the earth, whether we are searching for God or trying to understand where we belong?

The climate-change crisis reveals the price we have paid for not paying attention to our earth, our actual neighborhood where we live. When we look at our earth at the beginning of the twenty-first century, we see a planet in increasingly poor health. Moreover, we are not all in the same place on this planet: some of us are where things are still in fairly good condition, while others, most others (including other life-forms), are where things are falling apart. So when we ask where we are, what the neighborhood we live in is like, we have to differentiate between good neighborhoods and poor ones. The where question, the question of place and space, is also a question of justice—neglect of the neighborhood is undercutting the possibility of all its inhabitants living well.

Once we lower our eyes from the big heavenly questions—the why questions addressed by the classic Christian creation story—and look around at where we actually live, what our world is like, and how it can support all of us creatures decently, we realize that while the why questions will always interest us, it is the mundane where questions that may be more pressing. If "creation and providence" has less to do with questions of why things are the way they are and more to do with issues of where and how we live, then these issues would have to do not only with God and God's plans, but also and centrally with *who we are in the scheme of things and hence how we should behave*. If, for instance, the doctrine of creation was principally about *our place in nature*, then we would need to know a lot about the "natural world," how it functions to stay healthy, what its limits are, how its resources can be justly shared and permanently sustained. If we focused on one piece of the Genesis story, the piece that speaks of Adam and Eve being placed in the garden to care for it, we might have a different creation myth within which to find our place. Could one reason for human existence be simply "to care for the garden"? Were we created not to win salvation in another world, but to enjoy this one and help it to flourish? Could the goal of creation be the fulfillment of *all* God's creatures and not just the redemption of a few human creatures?

We will keep these questions in mind as we turn now to a typology of God-world relationships to see which views of creation and providence are both consonant with the Christian tradition and helpful for Christian thought and action in our time of climate change.

Models of God and the World

The Deistic Model

The first view that we will consider arose during the seventeenth-century scientific revolution. It imagines God as a clockmaker who winds up the clock of the world by creating its laws and then leaves it to run by itself, with the qualification that God intervenes periodically in natural disasters, accidents, and personal crises. The model has the advantage of freeing science to investigate the world apart from divine control, but it essentially banishes God from the world. Of the models we will look at, this deistic model separates God and the world most thoroughly—God is externally related to the world as a mechanic is to a machine. In this metaphor, the mechanic, after getting the machine going, only tinkers here and there when necessary. Strangely, this model—sterile, distant, and impersonal—is the one assumed by many contemporary Christians as well as nonbelievers. It is a convenient view for those who want to "keep religion out of business and politics," for those who do not wish a God who is immanent within creation and cares about its well-being. The deistic model says God is only minimally creator and caretaker of the world: this God has only to start it up, so to speak, and be present now and then in times of personal and public crisis. This model is neither Christian nor helpful for our twenty-first-century world. It knows nothing of the great Hebrew and Christian traditions of the compassionate, suffering, and always-present Emmanuel, the God with us, the one within whom the beloved creation is both rebuked and held in love. Moreover, this model is not relevant for our time: it appears totally ineffective in light of climate change. What sense does divine intervention make in a world of melting glaciers, species extinction, and growing human poverty?

The deistic model sees the world as totally secular, divorced from God—and from human beings, except as a "machine" for our use. The relationship between God and the world as well as between human beings and the world is utilitarian: we (and God) are "subjects," whereas the world and all its other creatures are "objects." This utilitarianism is in large measure why we are presently in our global warming crisis. It is interesting to note, however, that many scientists, especially biologists such as E. O. Wilson and Stephen Jay Gould, find that their study of the world ends in wonder and awe, not mere utilitarianism! This suggests, among other things, that the deistic model of God and the world is flat and uninteresting as well as non-Christian.

The Dialogic Model

The second view of God and the world has deep roots in both Hebrew and Christian traditions: God speaks, and we respond. It has been a central model within Protestantism and was highlighted in twentieth-century existentialism. In its contemporary form, the relation between God and the world is narrowed to God and the individual: the I-Thou relation between God and a human being. As seen, for instance, in the writings of Søren Kierkegaard and Rudolf Bultmann, this position focuses on sin, guilt, and forgiveness and has the advantage of allowing for a continuous relationship with God, but does so at the expense of indifference to the natural and social worlds. In its still more contemporary form, it embraces both born-again and certain New Age theologies: for born-again Christians, the God-world relationship is focused on the saved individual, while for some New Age adherents, it is limited to what comforts and satisfies the individual. In none of the above cases does creation include the natural and social worlds; rather, the "created" creature is almost exclusively human—and alone. This view, therefore, encourages an individualistic anthropology, which as we have seen is at the heart of our climate change crisis.

The dialogic position assumes two tracks, religion and culture (the latter including scientific knowledge and all social institutions such as government, the economy, and the family), with each left to run its own affairs. God and the human being meet not in the world (whether of culture or nature), but only in the internal joy and pain of human experiences. Whereas the deistic model keeps God and the world totally separate and externally related, the dialogic model allows them to touch, but only at one place, the inner human subject. Liberation theologies have protested the focus on individual alienation and despair, insisting that God's relation to the world must include the political and social dimensions as well. If the individual and the political worlds must be included in a credible doctrine of creation, how can we leave out the cosmos? What would a doctrine of creation be without *nature*? The difficulties with the dialogic position are obvious: it is too narrow, excluding nature from the God-world relationship and focusing fulfillment entirely on human individuals. This model is highly problematic in a time of climate change, for it blocks out everything except God and the human self. All models encourage us to see some things while at the same time excluding others. The dialogic model, of the several we are considering, excludes the world more completely than any of the others. Thus, it is a dangerous model for our time, although unfortunately it is highly popular as a form of personal spirituality.

The Monarchical Model

The third model sees the relation between God and the world as one in which the divine, all-powerful king controls his subjects, and they in turn offer him loyal obedience. It is the oldest of the models, the one that lies behind the traditional creation-providence story, and one that is still very popular. It is both a personal and a political model, correcting the impersonalism of the deistic model and the individualism of the dialogic. It also underscores the "godness" of God, for the monarchical imagery calls forth awe and reverence, as well as vocational meaningfulness, since membership in the kingdom entails service to the divine Lord. The continuing power of this model is curious since contemporary members of royalty scarcely call up responses of awe, reverence, and obedience, but its nostalgic appeal, as evidenced in the gusto with which we all sing Christmas carols that are rife with this imagery, cannot be underestimated. Any model that would attempt to criticize it ought to look carefully at the main reason for its attraction: it underscores and dramatizes divine transcendence. In other words, it accomplishes one of the tasks of a model of the God-world relationship: it emphasizes the power and glory of God.

Nonetheless, the monarchical model has several problems, the first being that the model of God as king depicts "domesticated" transcendence, for a king rules only over human beings, a minute fraction of created reality. In the king-realm model, God is neither genuinely transcendent (God is king over one species recently arrived on a minor planet in an ordinary galaxy) nor genuinely immanent (God as king is an external super-person, not the source, power, and goal of the entire universe). Moreover, a king is both distant from the natural world and indifferent to it, for the monarchical paradigm, as a political model, is limited to human beings. At most, nature enters this model only as the king's "realm" or "dominion," not with all the complexity, richness, and attention-grabbing qualities of the living, mysterious creation of which we are a part. Furthermore, the hierarchical nature of the model encourages human beings to act like kings in relation to the rest of creation: we are to subdue and dominate it.

The king-realm model would not be so harmful if it were not also hegemonic; that is, for many Christians, it (along with the father-child model) *describes* the divine-world relationship. It is not just *a* model—that is, one good, useful way of talking about the God-world relationship (while admitting there are other ways)—but *the* way. Both of these favorites, the king-realm and the father-child models, exclude the natural world; they exclude the neighborhood we need to pay attention to. Models are dangerous as well as helpful and necessary, for they allow us to see only what they want us to see. If the God-world relationship is not expressed in models that include the natural world—God's love for it and our responsibility for it—then we ignore it: the "world" will mean the human world, either personally or politically.

The Agential Model

The fourth model also is old, with strong backing in both the Hebrew and the Christian traditions. Here God is assumed to be an agent, a "person," whose intentions and purposes are realized in history. In its classical form, God is actor and doer, creator and redeemer of the world as well as its providential caretaker. God the personal agent oversees the world in every way, creating it from nothing; guiding it as father, lord, lover, king, protector; and, when it falls away like a wayward child, calling it back through divine sacrifice and compassion. This model obviously has contributed a great deal to the traditional creation-providence story; it, along with the king-realm model, is the backbone of that story, for it is the source of the overarching purposes and goals that are the story's structure. As we recall, in the traditional story, God creates the world for his own glory, apart from any need or desire. Creation is entirely a matter of divine intention—thus the enduring images of God as willing creation into existence through divine words ("Let there be . . .") and, like a potter, sculpting Adam from the clay. These images of creation come from God's "mind" and from God's "hands," from analogies with the way humans make and do things intentionally, with a purpose. In this model God is "like" us; the model underscores the humanlike qualities of God, especially those having to do with our ability to decide, influence, intend, and bring about actions, events, and conclusions.

One main difficulty with the agential model is that if God is like a personal agent who influences the world and brings it to its fulfillment, how does this take place? In earlier times, most ordinary people had little difficulty imagining God intervening in worldly events to direct and control them. Since the scientific revolution and especially postmodern evolutionary cosmology and biology, such ideas have become increasingly problematic. Such a God is an unnecessary intrusion in scientific explanation and has been marginalized to at most starting up the Big

Bang. While there have been efforts on the part of some theologians and scientists to internalize divine action within the cosmic processes and thus retain a notion of divine intention and design in nature, these efforts are aimed mainly at satisfying why, not where, questions; that is, they are aimed at allowing us to believe in both the existence of God and the truth of science. They are not oriented toward helping us learn about and pay attention to the world for its own flourishing; rather, they are meant to suggest that subtle, highly nuanced traces of divine purpose are evident in the world.[4]

Again, it is the "world" that is lacking in the agential model. The focus is on God and God's intentions for creation, how the divine will conceives, creates, saves, and brings to fulfillment everything that is. But the "everything that is" does not get much attention. The model is spiritual but not physical; it is about the mind but not the body. Nonetheless, this model is suggestive: What if the model was revised so that God as "person" would be not just mind, but also body? What if we did not insist on radical dualism between God and the world, with God being all spirit and the world being all matter or body, but imagined a model with God and the world being *both*? That is, what if the world were seen to be God's body, which is infused by, empowered by, loved by, given life by *God*? What if the world were seen to be "within" God, not identical with God (as our own bodies are not identical with us, for we can reflect about them, guide them, direct them, and so forth), but very intimately connected—sort of like a baby in the womb? Would such a model be a way of expressing profound interrelationship between God and the world, a way that might be closer to an incarnational understanding of the God-world relationship than are the other models we have considered? Would such a model also invite us to reflect on our responsibility for the world—the body of God—that is our home? Might it be a powerful model of the relation between God and the world in our context of climate change?

We will shortly consider this possibility in more detail, but before doing so, we need to remember that all models of God and the world are limited, partial, and imperfect. We are trying to get at the *most basic* expression of that relationship, realizing that there is no one right model, that many are needed, and that all have problems. If the most basic relationship for Christians is known in some way from the story of Jesus Christ, and if one interpretation of that story—perhaps its broadest and deepest interpretation—is that *God is with us here and now on our earth*, then which of the models we have considered is both Christian and appropriate for our time? Which model is better than the others—all that we can aim for—in expressing divine love for and presence in the world we actually inhabit? Is it the model of the clockmaker winding up the clock? The I-Thou model of God and an individual? The model of God as king and the world as his realm? The agential model of God acting in the world? Or the model of God as the spirit empowering the universe, the divine body? It is not necessary to choose only one of these models, but it probably is important to give priority to one, for the one we use as our main lens through which to view the God-world relationship will profoundly influence who we think we are in the scheme of things and how we behave in our world, our neighborhoods.

Creation and Providence in Light of the World as God's Body

We take as our text Augustine's words expressing his sense of the God-world relationship:

> Since nothing that is could exist without You, You must in some way be in all that is; [therefore also in me, since I am]. And if You are already in me, since otherwise I should not be, why do I cry to You to enter into me? . . . I should be nothing, utterly nothing, unless You were in me—or rather unless I were in You "of Whom and by Whom and in Whom are all things." So it is, Lord. So it is. Where do I call You to come to, since I am in You? Or where else are You that You can come to me? Where shall I go, beyond the bounds of heaven and earth, that God may come to me, since He has said: "Heaven and earth do I fill"?[5]

If God is always incarnate—if God is always in us and we in God— then Christians should attend to the model of the world as God's body.[6] For Christians, God did not become human on a whim; rather, it is God's nature to be embodied, to be the one in whom we live and move and have our being. In Christianity, the God-world relationship is understood in light of the incarnation; hence, creation is "like" the incarnation. Jesus Christ is the lens, the model, through whom Christians interpret God, the world, and themselves. The doctrine of creation for Christians, then, is not different in kind from the doctrine of the incarnation: in both, God is the source of all existence, the one *in whom* we are born and reborn. In this view, the world is not just matter while God is spirit; rather, there is a continuity (though not an identity) between God and the world. The world is flesh of God's "flesh"; the God who took our flesh in one person, Jesus of Nazareth, has always done so. God is incarnate, not secondarily but primarily. Therefore, an appropriate Christian model for understanding creation is the world as God's body. This is not a description of creation (there are no descriptions); neither is it necessarily the only model. It is, however, one model that is commensurate with the central Christian affirmation that God is with us in the flesh in Jesus Christ, and it is a model that is particularly appropriate for interpreting the Christian doctrine of creation in our time of climate change. Its merits and limitations should be considered in relation to other major models of the God-world relationship: God as clockmaker winding up the machine, as king of the realm, as father with wayward children, as personal agent acting in the world, and so forth.

The model of the world as God's body is appropriate for our time (as well as being in continuity with the Christian incarnational tradition) because it encourages us to focus on the neighborhood. It understands the doctrine of creation to be not primarily about God's power, but about God's love: how we can live together, all of us, within and for God's body. It focuses attention on the near, on the neighbor, on the earth, on meeting God not later in heaven but here and now. We meet God in the world and especially in the flesh of the world: in feeding the hungry, healing the sick—and in reducing greenhouse gases. An incarnational understanding of creation says nothing is too lowly, too physical, too mean a labor if it helps creation to flourish. We find God in caring for the garden, in loving the earth well: this becomes our vocation, our central task. Climate change, then, becomes a major religious, a major Christian, issue. To be a Christian in our time, one must respond to the consequences of global warming.

The doctrine of creation in this view is a practical, not an intellectual, affair. It is not about God's absolute power. The point of the doctrine is not to elevate God while demeaning us and the world; rather, it is to focus attention on our home, our garden planet. In Genesis,

God tells Adam and Eve not only to care for the garden, but also how good it is: after each act of creation in the first chapter of Genesis, God "saw that it was good." After completing the entire creation, "God saw everything that he had made, and indeed, it was very good" (Gen 1:31). Interestingly, God does not say that it is good for human beings or even good for me, God, but simply good. This is an aesthetic response expressing appreciation for the intrinsic value of each and every creature, plant, and planetary process (sun, moon, earth, water).

Hence, this understanding of creation asks us to find out about the neighborhood, so we can take care of it. It suggests that human beings are not the only creatures that matter; however, we are special. We are the caretakers, the ones who can help the garden flourish, help the body of God be well fed and healthy—or we can destroy it. We *know* the difference between good and evil: the unique characteristic of human beings, as well as our greatest burden, is that *we know that we know*. We not only know *how* to do many things (all animals know this), but we know that we *can* do many things and that some of these things are good and some bad for God's creation, God's body, our planetary garden. Climate change makes our responsibility for planetary health painfully evident. One of the most remarkable events of the early twenty-first century is global awakening to this fact.

Let us look more carefully at three implications of this model of creation and providence that are especially relevant for our context of global climate change. The implications of the model of the world as God's body are, first, that we must know our world and where we fit into it; second, that we must acknowledge God as the source of all life, love, truth, and goodness; and third, that we must realize that while God is in charge of the world, so are we.

Knowing the Body, Tending the Garden

In our model, the body of God is the entire universe; it is all matter in its myriad fantastic ancient and modern forms, from quarks to galaxies. More specifically, the body of God needing our attention is planet Earth, a tiny piece of divine embodiment that is our home and garden. In order to care for this garden, we need to know about it; in order to help all creatures who constitute this body flourish, we need to understand how we humans fit into this body.

All understandings of creation and providence rest on assumptions about what the world is like and where humans belong in it.

First-century Mediterranean, medieval, and eighteenth-century views of the world and the place of humans differ; the twenty-first-century view does as well. In our evolutionary, ecological view of reality, everything is interrelated and interdependent. As we have seen, "ecological unity" is both radically individualistic and radically relational. In an organism or body, the whole flourishes *only* when all of the different parts function well; in fact, the whole is nothing but each and every individual part doing its particular thing successfully. Nothing is more unified than a well-functioning body, but at the same time, nothing relies more on complex, diverse individuality.

Hence, the neighborhood in which we have been set down is one that we must learn to care for in all of its diverse parts and needs. We must become "ecologically literate," understanding the earth's most basic law: that there is no way the whole can flourish unless *all parts* are cared for. This means distributive justice is the key to sustainability; or, to phrase it differently, our garden home, the body of God, will be healthy long-term only if *all* parts of it are cared for appropriately. Before all else, the community, our planet, must survive (sustainability), which it can do only if all members have access to basic necessities (distributive justice). We need to learn "home economics," the basic rules of how our garden home can prosper—and what will destroy it. The science of global warming—its causes and effects—is one important piece of home economics whose rules we must learn and obey.

We must do so because, as the self-reflective part of God's body— the part that knows that we know—we have become partners with God in maintaining the health of creation, as climate change is making painfully clear. We are no longer the peak of creation, the one above all the others and for whom the others were made; rather, we are at one and the same time the neediest of all creatures and the most powerful. We cannot exist beyond a few minutes without air, a few days without water, or a few weeks without the plants, but we are also, given our population and high-energy lifestyle, the one species that can undermine the planet's well-being, as global warming, the decline of biodiversity, and the increasing gap between the rich and the poor are illustrating. In a strange paradox, we who have unprecedented power over the planet are at the same time at its mercy: if it does not thrive, neither can we.

As is evident, this first implication of the model of the world as God's body supports and underscores a radically ecological view of the world. It is entirely opposed to the cult of individualism endorsed by modern religion, government, and economics, all of which claim that human beings are basically separate, isolated individuals who enter into relationships when they wish. Perhaps the most important implication of creation as God's body is the new anthropology it demands: we are—basically, intrinsically, and always—interrelational, interdependent beings who live in total dependence on the others who compose the body, while at the same time we are responsible for the well-being of one tiny part of the body, planet Earth.

God as Source of Life and Love

A second implication of the model of creation as God's body is that it radicalizes both God's transcendence and God's immanence. This model has been criticized by some as pantheistic, as identifying God and the world. I do not believe it is. If God is to the universe as each of us is to our bodies, then God and the world are not identical. They are, however, intimate, internally related in ways that can make Christianity uncomfortable, when it forgets its incarnationalism. But we Christians should not shy away from a model that radically underscores both divine transcendence and divine immanence. How does it do so?

In the world as God's body, God is the source, the center, the spring, the spirit of all that lives and loves, all that is beautiful and true. When we say "God," that is what we mean: we mean the power and source of all reality. *We* are not the source of our own being; hence, we acknowledge the radical dependence on God of all that is. This is true transcendence: being the source of everything that is. Our universe, the body of God, is the reflection of God's being, God's glory; it is the sacrament of God's presence with us. The most radically transcendent understanding of God is, then, at the same time the most radically immanent understanding. Because God is always incarnational, always embodied, we can see God's transcendence *immanently*. Meeting God is not a momentary "spiritual" affair; rather, God is the ether, the reality, the body, the garden *in which we live*. God is never absent; God is reality (being). Everything that has being derives it from God (we are born of God and reborn by God). The entire cosmos is born of God, as is each and every creature. We depend on this source of life and its renewal absolutely. We could not live a moment without the gifts of God's body—air, food, water, land, and other creatures. This realization is an overwhelming experience of God's transcendence; it calls forth awe and immense gratitude. Yet at the same time, as Augustine puts it,

God is closer to us than we are to ourselves. Where can we go where God is not, since God fills heaven and earth? "I should be nothing, utterly nothing, unless You were in me—or rather unless I were in You." The God whom we meet through the earth is the source not only of my being, but of all being. We see glimmers of God in creation (God's body), and we see the same God more clearly in Jesus Christ, the major model of God for Christians.

The second implication of our model, then, is that it allows us to meet God in the garden, on the earth, at home. We do not have to go elsewhere or wait until we die or even be "religious." We meet God in the nitty-gritty of our regular lives, for God is always present in every here and now. This second implication underscores the first: since God is here in our world, then surely it is indeed our neighborhood, our planet and its creatures, that we should be caring for. The significance of the truth that the transcendent God is with us cannot be overestimated as we struggle to care for the earth. It means that we are not alone as we face the despair that creeps over us when at last we acknowledge our responsibility for climate change. We do not face this overwhelming problem on our own: God is with us as the source and power of all our efforts to live differently.

Who Is in Charge?

A third implication of our model of creation as God's body is that God alone is not in charge. Our model is not a mechanistic one: God does not control the world as a puppeteer controls puppets or a clock maker winds a clock or a king commands his subjects. Divine power is not unilateral—the more one party has, the less there is for the other. Rather, *God shares*: in organisms, power is mutual flourishing, empowerment, symbiosis. The whole does not flourish unless the parts are thriving. But this is messy business and does not result in the well-being of all creatures all the time—how could it? If the body of God is billions of different species and individuals, each one with a desire to live, there will inevitably be many that do not survive or flourish. An evolutionary, ecological picture of reality is not neat, nice, or romantic. It is indifferent, often brutal, and sometimes tragic. It also is often serendipitous: the same process that results in the AIDS virus or cancer cells created our brains and our emotions. Hence, so-called natural evil will occur—frequently and for no reason, depending on one's perspective (a flood helps some creatures and devastates others). However, natural evil, as global warming among other events is showing us, is seldom just "natural." Increasingly, we recognize that not only poverty is caused by human unwillingness to share resources justly, but even extreme weather events, including global temperature increase and its consequences, are due to human action. Thus, what the insurance companies used to call "acts of God" are no longer either divinely or naturally caused. Rather, in large part, *we* are causing them.

Add to "natural evil" what is called moral evil or sin: the perversions of reality (of life, love, goodness, beauty, truth) that we human beings perpetrate, both individually and collectively, and one has an awesome task for providence. A century that has known the Holocaust, Hiroshima, not to mention ordinary poverty, discrimination, and greed does not need to be told how powerful evil is. But in our model of the world as God's body, even these monstrous examples of evil do not imply "another" reality, an evil power, as it were. There is, in an incarnational creation story, only one reality: the world derives its being from God, lives within and toward God, and is "real" to the extent it reflects the one reality, God. Evil does not "exist." It does not have ontological status; rather, it is a perversion of good.[7] All that lives depends on God or comes from God; evil does not depend on God or come from God. This does not make it less powerful, less prevalent, or less tragic, but it does suggest that evil is not in charge, all appearances to the contrary. Christians believe that ultimately God is in charge: a doctrine of creation and providence without the resurrection would be a doctrine of despair. There is little in our world that suggests that God is in control; in fact, a quick scan of the daily newspaper headlines will easily refute this idea. Believing that God is in charge is "absurd." But perhaps believing in God is nothing more than trusting that God *is* in charge—no matter what happens. H. Richard Niebuhr says that believing in Jesus Christ means becoming suspicious of one's "own deep suspicion of the Determiner of Destiny."[8] Thus, in the model of the world as God's body, God does not control all events, but God is *in charge*. We are partners with God in helping the world to flourish—or we can contribute to its destruction as we are presently doing with climate change. But in ways we do not understand but believe to be true, *we* are not *finally* in charge: God is, so says the Yes of the resurrection.

We work out this faith here in our neighborhood. It is figuring out where we are even if we cannot know why we are here. If we see ourselves as within God's body, as tending the garden, as doing home economics for God's household, we can relax about some things and get busy with others. We can rest in the comfort of God's constant and enveloping presence, knowing that God holds the whole world in God's hands. We can, at the same time, get busy learning about our neighbors and how we can all live here justly and sustainably.

Conclusion: Creation or Redemption Christianity?

The model of the world as God's body suggests a creation-oriented Christianity in contrast to the tradition's heavy emphasis on redemption. In the end, there are many similarities between the two perspectives, for in each God is both creator *and* savior. However, the greatest difference between them is "where we are at home." In creation Christianity, we are at home here on the earth, an earth that exists within God. We may not know why we have been placed here, but we know where we are: we live within God. We live within God before we are born, during our time on earth, and after we die. We are always in the same place—within God.

In the other version of the Christian story, we are not at home on the earth. To be sure, God came to earth at one point, in the incarnation of the redeemer Jesus Christ, but otherwise God is only externally related to the world. In both stories we belong to God, but in the redemption-oriented one, we can find God only in and through Jesus Christ and the community founded by him. We are "at home" in the church, the body of Christ, but not in the world (which is not seen as the body of God). Our final home, where we really belong, is in another time and another place: we reach this world of eternal life through accepting Christ's reconciling death for our sins. Neither God nor we are at home on the earth; it is not where God is or where we (properly) belong.

But in the model of the world as God's body, there is only one world, our earth, which we inhabit and of which God is the source, spring, and power. God is primarily and always incarnated, and creation is the witness of that continuous presence with us. In Jesus of Nazareth, Christians believe God's embodied presence reaches its culmination; the implicit becomes explicit; the shadows of divine love and goodness, truth and beauty, move into the light. *We see the revelation of*

God in the face of Jesus Christ. In Jesus' ministry of feeding the hungry, healing the sick, and siding with the poor and oppressed—actions that countered conventional mores and led to his death—we see concretely what living rightly in God's body means. In the story of Jesus, we are brought face-to-face, as it were, with God's presence, a presence that we have always lived in and at times acknowledged. In this story, we learn two things about where we are: we are in God, and we are called to live as disciples of Jesus. We live within God; hence, we can relax and enjoy, for we are at home and there is no other place we want to be. We live also (and at the same time) on the earth; hence, we can get busy caring for our garden home. Moreover, the story of Jesus provides us with a vision of how we should care for this home in the kingdom of God, the eucharistic banquet, to which *all are invited to share the feast.* The story of ecological economics—home economics for planet Earth—provides us with a way to work toward that vision: through sharing resources with all creatures so earth may prosper (distributive justice for sustainability).

As we try to overcome our denial about climate change and accept the lifestyle changes at personal and public levels that it demands, we know that *we are not alone.* We live within God and with all the others who are called to share the feast. The human task, while awesome and frightening, is not ours alone—nature and God are there before us and with us. In closing, we recall the wonderful passage about the dry bones from the book of Ezekiel in which God asks the prophet, "Mortal, can these bones live?" Ezekiel, with what we can imagine was considerable hesitation if not incredulity, answers, "O Lord GOD, you know." Then God says, "Prophesy to these bones, and say to them: O dry bones, hear the word of the LORD. Thus says the Lord GOD to these bones: I will cause breath to enter you, and you shall live" (Ezek 37:3-5). And so we too ask, can these dry bones lives? Can our overheating, dry, and dying planet be healthy? In a way that recalls the creation of Adam in Genesis 2, God forms sinews, flesh, and skin onto the dry bones, reconstituting them into living beings. But in this creation, in contrast to the first one, God has two helpers: Ezekiel, who is the mediator of God's word that causes the bones to reassemble, and nature, the "four winds" that provide the breath that gives the bones life. To the question, can the power of life override the reality of death? the answer is yes, with the help of God's partners, human beings and nature itself.

5

HOW SHALL WE LIVE?
CHRISTIANITY and PLANETARY
ECONOMICS[1]

It is notable that none of the world's religions has as its maxim:
"Blessed are the greedy."
—Sallie McFague

We have looked at who we are and decided that an ecological anthropology is necessary for our contemporary context of global warming. It
is also commensurate with Christian faith. We have looked at who God
is and suggested that the model of the world as God's body might be a
persuasive contemporary and Christian expression for the God-world
relationship in our time. We have, then, sketched out a picture, a way of
imagining both ourselves and God within the context of radical environmental threat.

It is time now to look at how we should live. If we are interdependent with all other creatures as well as radically dependent on God, the
source of reality and goodness—who is transcendentally immanent in
the world and expects us to be partners in earthly flourishing—then
what should we do? Can we continue living in a way that consumes
the world's resources and undermines its most basic systems, as global

warming is warning us we are doing? Must we not see *the essential con-*
nection between economics and ecology: between the insatiable consumer
society and the wreckage it creates at all levels—resource depletion and
greenhouse gases, as well as a growing split between the poor and the
wealthy?

Religion and Economics

It is notable that none of the world's major religions has as its maxim:
"Blessed are the greedy." Given the many differences among religions
in doctrines and practice, it is remarkable to find such widespread
agreement at the level of economics. Often, however, people do not
consider that religion has anything to do with economics; in fact, in
most societies many do not want religion to intrude into economics. It
is preferable, they say, for religion to attend to "religious matters" and
to leave economics to the economists.

But most religions know better. They know that economics is
about human well-being, about who eats and who does not, who has
clothes and shelter and who does not, who has the basics for a decent
life and who does not. Economics is about life and death, as well as the
quality of life. It is also about the life and death not just of human beings but of the planet itself and all its life-forms. Economics is not just
about money; rather, it is about sharing scarce resources among all who
need them. Economics is a justice issue, so why would religions not be
concerned with it?

In many religions, the concern for justice has been focused on human beings—and this is certainly the case with Christianity, at least for
the last few centuries. But recently, the issues of well-being and justice
have been extended to embrace the entire planet: the well-being of
people and the well-being of the planet are increasingly seen to be inextricably related. Climate change makes this case with stunning clarity.
In Christianity, there is a return to the cosmological context for interpreting the faith, rather than the narrow psychological focus prevalent
since the Protestant Reformation. In fact, many current Christian theologies incorporate all three of the classical interpretive contexts: the
cosmological, the political, and the personal.[2] These theologies claim
that Christian faith embraces the *world*—all of creation and not just
we human beings who make up less than 1 percent of it. The redeemer

is also the creator: all of creation, including dying nature as well as oppressed people, is within God's "economy," God's "household."

As we have noted, it is no coincidence that the Greek word for house, *oikos*, is the source of our words *economics, ecology,* and *ecumenicity*. The three belong together: in order for the whole household of the planet to flourish, the earth's resources must be distributed justly among all its inhabitants, human and earth others, on a sustainable basis. This involves economics, for the distribution of scarce resources among needy users is the essence of economics. That economics and ecology are interconnected can be seen negatively in our consumer culture, which sets no limits on human consumption of resources—except monetary ones. Human beings, especially well-off ones, are permitted to consume all they can afford: no other criterion is applied. A market economy in a time of rising ecological destruction has no means of assuring that the third term—*ecumenicity*—will be included. Good "home economics" insists that the whole household must be fed now and in the future. As the effects of global warming accelerate, we see clearly that the economics being practiced globally is not contributing to a just, sustainable planet. What we need, instead, is an *ecological economics*.

But an economic paradigm based on ecological health is certainly not the dominant one in global society today. Nor is it the one that most Christians seem to be embracing. To be sure, Christians do not openly support the maxim "Blessed are the greedy"; nonetheless, that is the way most of us live. Why? Quite simply, because we are members of a society, now a worldwide one, that accepts, almost without question, an economic theory that supports insatiable greed on the part of individuals, regardless of its consequences to other people or to the planet. This assumption lies behind present-day market capitalism, and since the death of communism and the decline of socialism, it has been accepted by most ordinary people as a description of the ways things are and must be. It is "the truth." Although market capitalism is "a description of the way things are" in our society, it is not a description of the way things must be—or should be. Market capitalism is an economic *model*, not a description.[3] Market capitalism is a type of economics that allocates scarce resources not in regard to the needs of the planet's inhabitants nor with an eye to its sustainability, but rather on the basis of individuals' successful competition for them. Its criterion is who can pay. It is an economic theory that makes a case for the way scarce resources might be distributed, not how they must be.

This realization—that economics is not a hard science but an ideology with an assumed anthropology and a goal for the planet (summarized by greed and growth)—is the first step in seeing things otherwise. Ecological economics—economics for the well-being of the whole household of planet Earth—is also a model with an anthropological and planetary ideology. It claims that human beings, while greedy to be sure, are even more *needy*: we depend on the health of all the other parts of the planet for our very existence—clean water, breathable air, arable land, thriving plants, and so on. It claims that market capitalism denies one huge fact: unless the limited resources of the planet are distributed justly among all life-forms so they can flourish, there will be no sustainable future for even the greediest of us. Global warming is unmasking the presumed "objectivity" of market capitalism, for we see now that this model of economics is biased not in favor of the well-being of the whole planet, but in favor of a segment of the human population for its short-term gratification. Global warming is the stark evidence of the disaster that awaits us unless we shift swiftly and deeply to another form of economics.

Christianity and Economics

But why should Christians be concerned with models of economics? Is ecological economics "Christian"? No, but it is an emerging economic model that is gaining the support of a wide range of nongovernmental organizations (NGOs), protest movements, and people who believe an alternative economics is necessary. Its motto is "A different world is possible," and its basic tenets are concerned with fair labor laws and environmental health. Lynn White's oft-quoted 1967 essay lays the blame for environmental deterioration at the feet of religion, specifically Christianity.[4] If Christianity was capable of doing such immense damage, then surely the restoration of nature also must lie, at least in part, with Christianity. I believe it does, but also with other world religions as well as with education, government, and science. The environmental crisis we face—and which is epitomized by climate change—is a planetary agenda, involving all people, all areas of expertise, and all religions.

This is the case because the environmental crisis is not a "problem" that any specialization can solve, as climate change is increasingly demonstrating. Rather, it is about how we—all of us human beings and other creatures—can live justly and sustainably on our planet. Climate change is telling us that we must live differently. We need to pay attention to the "house rules" that will enable us to live as we ought. These house roles include attitudes as well as technologies, behaviors, and science. They are what the *oikos*, the house we all share, demands that we think and do so that there will be enough for everyone. The house rules are concerned with the management of the resources of planet Earth so that all may thrive indefinitely.

How does religion and specifically Christianity fit into this picture? It fits where all religions do: at the point of the worldview underlying the house rules.[5] It fits at the level of the deeply held and often largely unconscious assumptions about *who we are in the scheme of things and how we should act.*[6] While anthropology—the interpretation of human nature—is not the only concern of religions, it is a central one and, for the purposes of the ecological crisis, the one that may count the most.

I wish to make the case that Christianity, at least since the Protestant Reformation and especially since the Enlightenment, has through its individualistic view of human life supported the neoclassical economic paradigm, the current consumer culture, which is widening the gap between the rich and the poor and is a major cause of global warming. As an alternative, I suggest that Christianity should support an ecological economic model, one in which our well-being is seen as interrelated and interdependent with the well-being of all other living things and earth processes.[7] In other words, religions, and especially Christianity in Western culture, have a central role in forming *who we think we are and what we have the right to do.* The individualistic anthropology is deep within our consumer-oriented culture and is presently supported not only by religion but also by government and contemporary economics.[8] When these three major institutions—religion, government, and economics—present a united front, a "sacred canopy" is cast over a society, validating the behavior of its people. It is difficult to believe that science and technology alone can solve an ecological crisis supported by this triumvirate, for it legitimates human beings continuing *to feel, think, and act in ways that are basically contrary* to the just distribution of the world's resources and the sustainability of the planet itself.

Neoclassical
and Ecological Economics

The two worldviews—the neoclassical economic one and the ecological economic view—are dramatically different, suggesting different anthropologies and different house rules. The first model sees human beings on the planet as similar to a corporation or syndicate, a collection of individuals drawn together to benefit its members by optimal use of natural resources. The second model sees the planet more as an organism or a community, which survives and prospers through the interdependence of all its parts, human and nonhuman. The first model rests on assumptions from the eighteenth-century view of human beings as individuals with rights and responsibilities, and of the world as a machine or a collection of individual parts, related externally to one another. The second model rests on assumptions from postmodern science in its view of human beings as the conscious and radically dependent part of the planet, and of the world as a community or an organism, internally related in all its parts. *Both are models*, interpretations, of the world and our place in it; neither one is a description. This point must be underscored, because the first model seems "natural"—indeed, "inevitable" and "true"—to most middle-class Westerners, while the second model seems novel, perhaps even utopian or fanciful. In fact, both come from assumptions of different historical periods; both are world pictures built on these assumptions and each vies for our agreement and loyalty.

I will suggest that the corporation or machine model is injurious to nature and to poor people, while the other one, the community or organic model, is healthier for the planet and all its inhabitants. In other words, we need to assess the "economy" of both models, their notions of the allocation of scarce resources to family members, in order to determine which view of the "good life" is better.

The mention of "allocation of scarce resources" brings us to the heart of the matter. The reason economics is so important, the reason it is a religious and ecological issue, is that it is not just a matter of money; rather, it is a matter of survival and flourishing. Economics is a *value* issue. In making economic decisions, the bottom line is not the only consideration. Many other values are present in decisions concerning scarce resources and the way they should be deployed: from the health of a community to its recreational opportunities; from the beauty of other life-forms to our concern for their well-being; from a desire to see our children fed and clothed to a sense of responsibility for the welfare of future generations. Climate change is intimately involved in this value issue: one of the reasons global warming is occurring is our preference to make money through excessive consumption regardless of the consequences to the planet.

Contemporary neoclassical economists, however, generally deny that economics is about values.[9] But this denial is questionable. By neoclassical economics, we mean market capitalism as conceived by Adam Smith in the eighteenth century and, more particularly, the version of it practiced by major economies of our time. The key feature of market capitalism is the allocation of scarce resources by means of decentralized markets: allocation occurs as the result of individual market transactions, each of which is guided by self-interest.[10] At the base of neoclassical economics is an anthropology: human beings are individuals motivated by self-interest. The value by which scarce resources are allocated, then, is the fulfillment of the self-interest of human beings. The assumption is that everyone will act to maximize his or her own interest, and by so doing all will eventually benefit—the so-called invisible hand of classical economic theory.

Neoclassical economics has *one* value: the monetary fulfillment of individuals provided they compete successfully for the resources. But what of other values? Two key ones, if we have the economics of the entire planet in mind, are the just distribution of the earth's resources to all needy users and the ability of the planet to sustain our use of its resources. However, these matters—distributive justice to the world's inhabitants and the optimal scale of the human economy within the planet's economy—are considered "externalities" by neoclassical economics.[11] In other words, the issues of who benefits from an economic system and whether the planet can bear the system's burden are not part of neoclassical economics.

These so-called externalities are, in fact, not minor or extraneous matters. On the contrary, as climate change is illustrating, they are the heart of the matter. For example, environmental deterioration, a prime "externality," is not figured into the price of goods in market capitalism. A company may have to pay a penalty for ecological damage—as in the oil spill from the *Exxon Valdez*—but it did not have to include in the price of the oil the greenhouse gas emissions caused by its initial production. Other "externalities" include the issues of justice and sustainability, as well as recreational and aesthetic values. None of these matters counts in the price tag according to market capitalism.

In sum, the worldview of neoclassical economics is surprisingly simple and straightforward: the crucial assumption is that human beings are self-interested individuals who, acting on this basis, will create a syndicate, even a global one, capable of benefiting all eventually. Hence, as long as the economy grows, individuals in a society will sooner or later participate in prosperity. These assumptions about human beings are scarcely value-neutral. They indicate a preference for a certain view of who we are and what the goal of human effort should be: the view of human nature is individualism, and the goal is growth. Neither human poverty nor nature's deterioration has a place in this model of economics—and certainly not the issue of climate change.

When we turn to the alternative ecological economic paradigm, we see a different set of values. Are we basically greedy or needy? Probably both, but as our answers veer toward one pole or the other, we will find ourselves embracing an individualistic or a communitarian model of life. Ecological economics claims that we cannot survive (even to be greedy) unless we acknowledge our profound dependence on one another and on the earth. Human need is more basic than human greed: we *are* relational beings from the moment of our conception to our last breath. The well-being of the individual is inextricably connected to the well-being of the whole.

These two interpretations of who we are and where we fit in the world are almost mirror opposites of each other on the three critical issues of allocation of resources, distributive justice, and sustainability. Neoclassical economics begins with the unconstrained allocation of resources to competing individuals, on the assumption that if all people operate from this base, issues of distribution and sustainability will eventually work themselves out. Ecological economics begins with the viability of the whole community, on the assumption that only as it thrives now and in the future will its various members, including human beings, thrive as well. In other words, ecological economics *begins* with sustainability and distributive justice, not with the allocation of resources among competing individuals. Before all else, the community must be able to survive (sustainability), which it can do only if all members have the use of resources (distributive justice). Then, within these parameters, the allocation of scarce resources among competing users can take place.

Ecological economics does not pretend to be value free; its preference is evident—the well-being and sustainability of the whole household, planet Earth. It recognizes the *oikos* base of ecology, economics, and ecumenicity: *economics is the management of a community's physical necessities for the benefit of all.* Here we see the tight connection between economics and ecology—and in our present situation, the connection between market economics and global warming. Climate change clearly shows that neoclassical economics is a failure in managing the planet's resources for the benefit of all. Ecological economics, on the other hand, is a human enterprise that seeks to maximize the optimal functioning of the planet's gifts and services for all users. Ecological economics, then, is first of all a vision of how human beings ought to live on planet Earth in light of the perceived reality of where and how we do in fact live. *We live in, with, and from the earth.* This story of who we are is based on postmodern science—not, as in neoclassical economics, on the eighteenth-century story of reality—a story that eliminated nature as a major player.

Neoclassical or Ecological Economics: Which Is Good for Planet Earth?

In answering this question, we are asking about the most important of the three economic issues: sustainability, with climate change as our case study. Can neoclassical economics as currently understood sustain the planet? In the neoclassical economic view, the "world" is a machine or a collection of individuals; presumably, then, when some parts give out, they can be replaced with substitutes. If, for instance, our main ecological problem is the scarcity of nonrenewable resources (oil, coal, minerals, and so forth), then human ingenuity might well fill the gaps when shortages occur.

The problem facing our planet at the beginning of the new millennium, however, is far greater than simply the loss of nonrenewable resources. In fact, that problem is of less importance than two other related ones: the rate of loss of *renewable* resources and the manner in which these losses overlap and support further deterioration. As we noted in chapter 1, when an organic-like entity, such as the earth, undergoes change, everything is affected—and the change snowballs. The big problems are the loss of water, trees, fertile soil, clean air, fisheries, and biodiversity *and* the ways the degradation of each of these renewables contributes to the deterioration of the rest. In other words, if the planet is seen more as an organism than a machine, with all parts interrelated and interdependent, then after a certain level of decay of its various members, it will, like any "body," become sick at its core, sick to the point of not functioning properly. It will not be able to sustain itself. We have already noted this phenomenon in our discussion of the "tipping point" of global temperature, an increase of such proportions that the life-sustaining systems of the planet are undermined.

This process refers to the *synergism* of planetary operation. The various parts of the planet work together both in health and in decay to create something either better or worse than the individual parts. When the various members of an ecosystem are healthy, they work together to provide innumerable "free services" that none could provide alone, services that we usually take for granted: materials production (food, fisheries, timber, genetic resources, medicines), pollination, biological control of pests and diseases, habitat and refuge, water supply and regulation, waste recycling and pollution control, educational and scientific resources, and recreation.[12] These services are essential to our survival and well-being; they can continue only if we sustain them. This list of services should be seen as a web: none of them can function alone—each of them depends on the others. These services are the "commons" that is our very lifeblood and that we hold in trust for future generations.

The most important services are not necessarily the most visible ones; for instance, in a forest it is not only the standing trees that are valuable but also the fallen ones (the "nurse logs" on which new trees grow); the habitat the forest provides for birds and insects that pollinate crops and destroy diseases; the plants that provide biodiversity for food and medicines; the forest canopy that breaks the force of winds; the roots that reduce soil erosion; the photosynthesis of plants that help stabilize the climate. The smallest providers—the insects, worms, spiders, fungi, algae, and bacteria—are critically important in creating a stable, sustainable home for humans and other creatures. If such a forest is clear-cut, everything else goes as well. Or, in a situation such as the extreme deterioration that climate change will create, *all of these services will disappear as well.* A healthy ecosystem—complex and diverse in all its features, both large and small—is resilient like a well-functioning body. A simplified, degraded nature, supporting single-species crops in ruined soil with inadequate water and violent weather events, results in a diminished environment for human beings as well. "The bottom line is that for humans to be healthy and resilient, nature must be too."[13]

An outstanding example of *negative* synergy is global warming, which undermines all of the wonderful "free services" nature gives us when it is healthy. Over the past two hundred years since the Industrial Revolution and the sharp increase of carbon dioxide emissions, we have seen a gradual unraveling of the billions of complex threads—flora and fauna, systems and processes—that work together to create the intricately patterned "cloak of life" that covers our earth. When we list the effects of global warming, we must remember more than just the most visible ones, such as desertification of grain-producing lands, scarcity of fresh water, loss of trees, flooding of coastal lands and islands, the spread of tropical diseases, torrid temperatures, and the decline of biodiversity. It is what we don't see in negative synergy that is crucial: the way that a whole healthy system is undermined as the threads that constitute the fabric unravel. We not only lose polar bears with global warming; we lose the entire Arctic climate system that supports polar bears—and so much more. Through our high-energy consumer lifestyle, we have triggered fearful, though still not fully understood, consequences for the most important and sensitive systems within which we and everything else exist. Global warming is a canary in the mine; the deterioration and death it is bringing are the signal that our lifestyle lies outside the planet's house rules.

An economic model that does not have as its first priority the sustainability of the planet cannot be good for human beings. The neoclassical economic model does not have such a priority. Hence, it is not good for us *even if we like it*—and we do like it. We are addicted to our consumer lifestyle and are only beginning to wake up to how bad it is for us and for the planet.

Christianity and the Ecological Economic Model

The model we need is very different. To recall, the ecological model claims that housemates must abide by three main rules: (1) Take only your share. (2) Clean up after yourself. (3) Keep the house in good repair for future occupants. We need to abide by these rules at personal, societal, and global levels. We don't own this house; we don't even rent it. It is loaned to us "free" for our lifetime with the proviso that we obey the above rules so that it can continue to feed, shelter, nurture, and delight others. These rules are not laws that we can circumvent or disobey; they are the conditions of our existence, and they are intrinsic to our happiness. If we were to follow these rules, we would be living within a different vision of the good life, the abundant life, than the current vision in our consumer culture that is destroying the planet.

Given these two economic worldviews—the neoclassical and the ecological—which should Christianity support? Presently, it is support-ing the neoclassical economic paradigm *to the degree that it does not speak against it and side publicly with the ecological view.* Does this matter? Yes, if one accepts the assumption that worldviews matter. While there is no direct connection between believing and acting, thinking and doing, there is an implicit, deeper, and more insidious one: the worldview that persuades us it is "natural" and "inevitable" becomes the secret partner of our decisions and actions.

Moreover, a persuasive case can be made that there is an intrinsic connection between the ecological economic model and Christianity. Distributive justice and sustainability, as goals for planetary living, are pale reflections, but reflections, nonetheless, of what Jesus meant by the kingdom of God.[14] In chapter 2, we looked briefly at the portrait of Jesus by New Testament scholar John Dominic Crossan.[15] Let us look at it again and more deeply: "The open commensality and radical egalitari-anism of Jesus' Kingdom of God are more terrifying than anything we have ever imagined, and even if we can never accept it, we should not explain it away as something else."[16] For Jesus, the kingdom of God was epitomized by *everyone* being invited to the table. *The kingdom is known by radical equality at the level of bodily needs.* Crossan names the parable of the feast as central to understanding what Jesus meant by the king-dom of God. This is a shocking story, trespassing society's boundaries of class, gender, status, and ethnicity—since its end result is the invita-tion of *all* to the feast. There are several versions (Matt 22:1-13; Luke 14:15-24; *Gos. Thom.* 64), but in each a prominent person invites other, presumably worthy, people to a banquet, only to have them refuse: one to survey a land purchase, another to try out some new oxen, a third to attend a wedding. The frustrated host then tells his servants to go out into the streets of the city and bring whomever they find to dinner: the poor, maimed, blind, lame, good, and bad (the list varies in the three ver-sions). The shocking implication is that everyone—*anyone*—is invited. As Crossan remarks, if beggars came to your door, you might give them food or even invite them into the kitchen for a meal, but you wouldn't ask them to join the family in the dining room or invite them back on Saturday night for supper with your friends.[17] But that is exactly what happens in this story. The kingdom of God, according to this portrait of Jesus, is "more terrifying than anything we have ever imagined" because it demolishes all of our carefully constructed boundaries between the worthy and the unworthy and does so at the most physical, bodily level.

For first-century Jews, the key boundary was purity laws: one did not eat with the poor, women, the diseased, or the "unrighteous." For us in our consumer society, the critical barrier is economic laws: one is not called to sustainable and just sharing of resources with the poor, the disadvantaged, the "lazy." To do otherwise in both cultures is improper; it is not expected—in fact, it is shocking. And yet in both cases, the issue is the most basic bodily one—who is invited to share the food. In other words, the issue is who lives and who dies. In both cases, the answer is the same: everyone, regardless of status (by any criteria), is invited. This vision of God's will for the world does not specifically mention just, sustainable planetary living, but it surely is more in line with that worldview than with the worldview based on the satisfaction of individual consumer desires.

Unlike our first-century Mediterranean counterparts, North American middle-class Christians are not terrified by the unclean, but we are terrified by the poor. There are so many of them—billions! Surely we cannot be expected to share the planet's resources justly and sustainably with all of them. Climate change is making this terror very clear: it demands basic changes in our economic policies toward greater egalitarianism at all levels. It demands that we think of the "body" of the world and what it needs in order to flourish, rather than focusing on our own consumer desires. One of the principal reasons for global warming denial is the realization that "everyone is invited" to the table of household Earth—including not just needy human beings, but the air, the water, the land, and each and every creature, no matter how small and seemingly insignificant. The terror implicit in this parable lies with its radical inclusivity—nothing, no one, is left out. "The Kingdom of God . . . began at the level of the body and appeared as a shared community of healing and eating—that is to say, of spiritual and physical resources available to each and all without discrimination, or hierarchies."[18]

The body is the locus: how we treat needy bodies gives the clue to how a society is organized. It suggests that correct "table manners" are a sign of a just society, the kingdom of God. If one accepts this interpretation, the "table" becomes not primarily the priestly consecrated bread and wine of Communion celebrating Jesus' death for the sins of the world, but rather the egalitarian meals of bread and fish that one finds throughout Jesus' ministry.[19] At these events, all are invited, with no authoritarian brokering, to share in the food, whether it be meager or sumptuous. Were such an understanding of the Eucharist to infiltrate Christian churches today, it could be mind-changing—in fact, world-changing. The parable of the feast is a metaphor for Christians encountering climate change because *it focuses on the body and its needs.* It reminds us that our planet is a deteriorating body in desperate need, and only as we begin to live differently—to live by its house rules of just distribution and sustainability—will we begin to respond appropriately to the crisis.

If this is the case, then for middle-class North American Christians, it may well be that *sin* is refusing to acknowledge the link between the kingdom and the ecological economic worldview, denying it because of the consequences to our privileged lifestyle. Sustainability and the just distribution of resources are concerned with human and planetary well-being *for all.* This proposition is indeed terrifying, but it is not absurd. In fact, it is, I suggest, the responsible interpretation of the parable of the feast for twenty-first-century well-off North American Christians. It demands that we look at the behaviors and systemic structures that are causing poverty and ecological deterioration in our world and name these behaviors and structures for what they are: evil. They are the collective forms of "our sin." They are the assumptions, institutions, and laws of market capitalism (often aided by the silence of the churches) that allow people and the planet to become impoverished. Our sin is one of commission, but perhaps more damningly of omission: our greed camouflaged by indifference and denial, while at the same time we offer charity to the poor and green rhetoric to "the environment."

Next Steps: A Christian Response

To dislodge the neoclassical economic worldview and Christianity's complicity with it, we must take four steps.

The first step is to become conscious that neoclassical economics is a model, not a description, of how to allocate scarce resources. There are other ways to live, other ways to divide things up, other goals for human beings and the planet. "Economics" is always necessary, but not necessarily neoclassical economics: ecological economics is an alternative. Since the death of communism and the retreat of socialism, religious worldviews are one of the few sources left to critique the hegemony of market capitalism. Without the presence of alternative visions, a model becomes an ideology, as market capitalism has become in our time.

A second step is to suggest some visions of the good life that are not consumer dominated, visions that are just and sustainable. The good life is not necessarily the consumer life; rather, it could include the basic necessities for all, universal medical care and education, opportunities for creativity and meaningful work, time for family and friends, green spaces in cities and wilderness for other creatures. We need to ask what *really* makes people happy and which of these visions are just for the world's inhabitants and sustainable for the planet.

A third step is for well-off Christians as well as others to publicly advocate the ecological model as a more just and sustainable one for our planet—and as the model that climate change is demanding we accept. While the ecological model is not the kingdom of God, Christians have the obligation to work for systems that are at least faint approximations of the kingdom, rather than clear opponents. Specifically, this means becoming informed about the global injustices of market economies; joining with other NGOs to change the policies and practices of so-called free trade that result in impoverishment and unsustainability; and accepting the consequences for one's own lifestyle that sharing earth's resources justly and sustainably will entail. It means also acknowledging the tight connection between market economics and global warming: unlimited consumerism is a major contributor to greenhouse gases.

The fourth step is to rethink what such a different context—the ecological economic one—would mean for the basic doctrines of Christianity: God and the world, Christ and salvation, human life and discipleship. Such reconstruction is the central task of this book, but here we will close the chapter with a few brief comments summing up the picture of God and the world that has emerged so far. This picture is at the heart of *who we think we are and what we should do*. Since our interpretive context, the ecological economic model, is about the just and sustainable allocation of resources in our time of climate change, the framework for speaking of God and the world becomes worldly well-being. Dietrich Bonhoeffer called it "worldly Christianity": he said that God is neither a metaphysical abstraction nor the answer to gaps in our knowledge—God is neither in the sky nor on the fringes, but at "the center of the village," in the midst of life, both its pains and its joys.[20] This is an earthly God, an incarnate God, who cares about the flourishing of creation.

As we look at the general outline of this theology, we find that it is basically different from the theology implied by the neoclassical model. Broadly speaking, the differences can be suggested as *a movement toward the earth*: from heaven to earth; from otherworldly to this-worldly; from above to below; from a distant, external God to a near, immanent God; from time and history to space and land; from soul to body; from individualism to community; from mechanistic to organic thinking; from spiritual salvation to holistic well-being; from anthropocentrism to cosmocentrism. The ecological model means a shift *not* from God to the world, but from a distant God related externally to the world to an embodied God who is the source of the world's life and fulfillment. The neoclassical model assumes God, like a human being, is an individual, in fact, the super-individual who controls the world through laws of nature, much as a good mechanic makes a well-designed machine operate efficiently. This God is at the beginning (creation) and intervenes from time to time to influence personal and public history, but otherwise is absent from the world. The ecological model, on the contrary, claims that God is radically present in the world, as close as the breath, the joy, and the suffering of every creature. The two views of God and the world, then, are very different: in the one, God's power is evident in God's distant control of the world; in the other, God's glory is manifest in God's total self-giving to the world.

In closing, let us note that the two pictures of God and the world suggest different answers to the question we have been pursuing in this book: Who are we, and what should we do? In the first view, we are individuals responsible to a transcendent God who rewards and punishes us according to our merits and God's mercy. In the second view, we are beings-in-community living in the presence of God, who is the power and love in everything that exists. In the first, we should do what is fair to other individuals while taking care of our own well-being; in the second, we should do what is necessary to work with God to create a just and sustainable planet, for only in this way will all flourish.

A just and sustainable planet is the great work of the twenty-first century to which all religions—indeed, all areas of human endeavor—are called. The crisis of climate change is making the necessity of this common task crystal clear. It is no longer debatable. But we are neither left alone to do this work nor ignorant of what needs to be done. God is with us—closer to each and every creature than we can ask or imag- ine—and we have some clues on how to proceed—in the kingdom of God and its pale reflection, the ecological economic model. Thanks be to God!

PART THREE

Serving God and
Living in the *City*
within *Climate Change*

6

WHY WE WORSHIP: PRAISE and COMPASSION as INTIMATIONS of TRANSCENDENCE

Being here is magnificent.
—Rainer Maria Rilke

What kind of religious response to climate change is possible within the confines of postmodernism? Postmodernism questions religion's focus on belief in the existence of God rather than action for the world. Is religion primarily about God-talk, or is it about loving the world? John Caputo expresses this critique precisely:

> When we pondered the translatability or substitut-
> ability of these two terms, "God" and "love," and
> we asked which is a translation of which, we were
> looking in the wrong place for a translation. In the
> translatability of the love of God it is *we* who are
> to be translated, transformed, and carried over into
> action, carried off by the movements of love, carried
> away by the transcendence that this name names
> and commands. The translation of the love of God is

transcendence; it is the movement that it names, the deed that it demands, for the love of God is something to *do*.[1]

"Transcendence" is not primarily about God; rather, transcendence is the movement, the deed, that we do "for the love of God." Could we then say that to praise God and to love neighbor are intimations of transcendence, of "religion"? Religion is not primarily about belief in the existence of God; rather, religion is about *doing* something, enacting love in the world. As Caputo quips, "My 'responsibility' is not just to speculate at my word processor about the name of God but to *do* justice."[2]

If we were to limit ourselves to such an understanding of religion—to bracket questions of God's existence and our belief in such existence—what would be left? Would we have a form of religion that could address the deep change in sensibility needed to fight climate change? Would we have a form of Christianity that could do so? If we put aside the issues of belief and focused on a phenomenological view of religion—on what most religious people *do*—could we see a strong role for the religions in the climate change agenda? I believe we would, and this chapter is an experiment reflecting on religion and climate change within the limits of deconstruction.

Praising God and Loving Neighbor

Humility is the only permitted form of self-love. Praise for God, compassion for creatures, humility for oneself.
—Simone Weil[3]

And now faith, hope, and love abide, these three; and the greatest of these is love.
—1 Cor 13:13

The two most distinctive activities of religious people are gratitude toward God and compassion toward others. The most prevalent religious emotion does not appear to be fear, but thanksgiving. A sense of gratitude seems to well up in us, even in those who are not "religious." We nod in agreement when Annie Dillard writes, "I go my way, and my left foot says 'Glory,' and my right foot says 'Amen,'"[4] or when Rilke exclaims, "Being here is magnificent." Indeed it is. It is also horrible and horrifying, from the reckless waste and bloody violence of nature's ways to the even more shocking perversion of human greed and hatred. What climate change will add to this picture of beauty lost and species gone extinct stretches the imagination. It forces us to recognize, admire, and grieve what we take for granted. We live in a terrifying, wonderful world, and in the midst of it, some people, many people, end up full of praise, feeling blessed and wanting to bless. People as various as Job and Francis of Assisi do; so does the writer of Psalm 104 ("I will sing to the LORD as long as I live," v. 33) and Gerard Manley Hopkins ("The world is charged with the grandeur of God"); and so do two nonbelieving biologists—E. O. Wilson, who wrote that "biophilia" is a natural human emotion, and Stephen Jay Gould, who said that evolution could be described with the movie title *A Wonderful Life*.[5] Dillard puts it this way: "The canary . . . sings on the skull."[6]

It seems that in all religious traditions, and outside them as well, gratitude and delight emerge from human beings, spilling out from us in exorbitant words of praise. Is this phenomenon an intimation of transcendence? I do not know, but all this language cannot simply be ignored or rejected. Deconstructionists Jean-Luc Marion and Jacques Derrida acknowledge this language in their discussions on the "gift" as the impossible possibility—what we most desire but can never have short of idolatry.[7] They acknowledge it, however, in a minimalist way (and for good reasons as they have argued). But is this sufficient to account for the depth and breadth of the language of exorbitant praise? Whether we look at the writings of mystics of all traditions, the Islamic poets, the Hindu sacred scriptures, the psalms of the Hebrew scriptures, or the religious ceremonies of Indigenous Peoples—or even the theologies of such Christians like Irenaeus, Augustine, Thomas Aquinas, Pierre Teilhard de Chardin, and Elizabeth Johnson—we find a huge discourse of thanksgiving. Even many so-called nonbelievers, who are aware that they did not create themselves and are just grateful to be alive, use such language. One way of describing this discourse is with the ancient term *via positiva*, the way of affirmation, but that is not entirely accurate. This language is not intended to describe God as much as it is meant to express a sense of trust, what Paul calls "faith" and what Weil calls "praise." It is the acknowledgment of a way of being in the world, one in which gratitude and humility seem like the most appropriate stances, regardless of "belief in God."

Hence, the first thing I want to suggest is that we take this language seriously. Here one should not be minimalist but should let out all the stops: there is no praise too great, no language too extravagant for expressing our yes to the gift of life, in spite of the shocking negativities and evils it involves. It is a gesture, a thank-you, that wells up from human beings in the most likely and unlikely places, from moments of exquisite joy (the birth of a child) to times of excruciating pain (the death of a child). Is it an intimation of transcendence?

Another place where transcendence may be found is in compassion, the practice of love. Is the Augustinian conversion of "God is love" into "Love is God" suggesting that love of neighbor and not praise to God is primary?[8] Is love for the other, particularly the other in lowercase, the heart of religion as well as the *primary* intimation of transcendence? It may well be. As we have noted, there is not a single religion in the world that has as its commandment: "Blessed are the greedy." In fact, there is almost universal agreement concerning the importance of self-limitation and self-abnegation so that others may live and prosper. The language of doing, of love, certainly is taken seriously by deconstruction. Both Derrida and Emmanuel Levinas, as well as the Hebrew scriptures and Judaism, focus on the good deed. This is a welcome direction after centuries of Christian and especially Protestant obsession with belief in God as the primary issue. The deconstructionists are correct, I think, in claiming that, as John Caputo puts it, "the name of God is the name of a deed."[9] In this way, the central project of religion is grounded in ethics, not theology. Issues of the existence and nature of God, which have been the focus of Western Christianity, now become secondary, as do ontology and metaphysics. The distinctive activity of religious people is not agony over the existence or nonexistence of God. This seems to be a peculiar activity, a special concern, of Western Christian theologians who are, after all, a minor voice relative to the approximately six billion people who belong to one of the world's ten thousand or so religions. Most of these people spend more time thanking God and trying to live as God wishes than they do worrying about God's existence.[10] Moreover, need transcendence mean "God's existence"—a being or the highest being—that exists apart from the world and is in control of the world? Might intimations of divine transcendence be hidden within human praise and compassion, those strange countercultural activities of religious (and other) people, those activities of thankfulness, even when the world is a thankless place, and of love for others, even when such deeds are contrary to the market capitalist ethic of self-fulfillment?

Now, of course, I have no firm evidence for these outrageous suggestions. They ring true in terms of my own experience, and I notice them elsewhere in saints and ordinary people in my own religious tradition and in others. But they are merely anecdotal. Failing being able to prove them, I would at least like to play with their possibility for a while. More specifically, I would like to play with the model of the world as God's body as a way of filling out how praise and compassion might be intimations of transcendence for postmodern Christians. I would like to suggest that an interpretation of Christian faith that focuses on the earth as where God is and where we are holds special insight into how we should "be religious" in a time of radical climate change.

The model of the world as God's body grounds Christian praise and doing in the ordinary, physical world. It suggests that the conventional meaning of transcendence as other than this world, beyond and separate from this world, is subverted into transcendence as radical immanence. It dares to make this move on the basis of the Christian assertion that the Word was made flesh, that God is incarnate in the world. It radicalizes the orthodox belief that Jesus of Nazareth alone is the Word made flesh by imagining the world—all of creation—as God's body. Incarnationalism means that transcendence becomes radical immanence. Christians are invited to imagine the entire universe—all matter and energy in their billions of differentiated forms—as God with us or, more accurately, as the body, the matrix, in which we live and move and have our being. With a sharp turn from the Barthian notion of transcendence as God relating to the world only as a tangent touches a circle, the model of the world as God's body suggests that God is the milieu in which we exist—exist at all levels and in all ways, but in ways that begin and end with the *body*. This model asks us to play with the possibility that Christianity is not about two worlds—the transcendent, heavenly one where we really belong (and where God abides) and the immanent, earthly one where we work out our salvation in sin and sorrow (and from which God is absent). Rather, the world as God's body suggests that there is *one* world, one reality, and this world, this reality, is divine. The divine is physical (as well as spiritual), as we—all of us—are. There is no absolute line dividing matter and spirit, body and soul, nature and humanity, or the world and God. Contemporary science tells us this, but it is also the heart of incarnational thinking. The model of the world as God's body suggests a creation theology of praise to God and compassion for the world in contrast to Christian theologies of redemption that focus on sin and on escape from the world.[11]

How, more specifically, is the model of the world as God's body a way of speaking of transcendence in Christian terms? How are praise and compassion, when focused on the world's body, intimations of transcendence? Two central issues are posed here. First, what is the status of metaphorical language for God-talk? What kind of assertions does it make? Is it a form of onto-theology? Does it limit itself to appropriate human humility and minimalism? Are metaphorical statements different from analogical and symbolic ones? Second, what kind of transcendence is suggested by body language? How can what is radically immanent (the body) be the place of transcendence? How would we praise God and serve our neighbor differently if we were to do so within the model of the world as God's body?

We will, therefore, be attending to two issues: the status of metaphor as a way to speak of transcendence, and the ways in which praise and compassion are intimations of transcendence when practiced within the model of the world as God's body. To state my thesis in its bare bones, I turn to Exod 33:23: "And you shall see my back; but my face shall not be seen." We do not know God or see God. What we know and see is what Moses saw—the "back" of God, the body of God, which is the world. Through this mediation of God via the world, we praise God *using the world* to do so, since we have no other means. Likewise, we care for and have compassion for our world, God's body, in all its needs, especially the most physical ones including food, water, home, and health. A thoroughly incarnational—or "back side"—theology accepts the limitations of our earthly, bodily existence, finding intimations of transcendence *in and through* the world, intimations that at times cause us to say "thank you" and to mean it. At other times, they impel us to pay attention to others, to their most basic needs, their bodily needs. Such intimations of transcendence are small and modest. Moreover, they are by no means the only intimations—just bodily ones. By encouraging us to look through the filter of physicality in seeking for God, they highlight the sensuous, bodily, physical, basic aspects of life while blocking out many others. The body metaphor is an important one; it is by no means the only one and must be complemented by others. Finally, functioning within metaphor, this theology can make few pretensions to metaphysical assertions. As Derrida and many others have pointed out, metaphor lies between nonsense and truth.[12] Indeed it does. Metaphor says that the world is/*is not* God's body. All it asks is that we entertain the nonsense for a while in order to see if there is any truth in it.

We are attempting to see if a minimalist Christian theology, one that avoids metaphysical claims, can contribute to the sensibility needed for dealing with climate change. Were we to stay with modest metaphorical statements and to focus on the "body," the world as God's body as well as all the millions of bodies that constitute our earth, would we have the makings of a religious and ethical response sufficient to fight global warming? Would a deepening sense of praise for the beauty of the earth as well as a more profound compassion for its vulnerability be appropriate and powerful intimations of transcendence for us at this time? Would a body theology and ethic perhaps be exactly what a world facing climate change needs?

Metaphor and Model as the Language of Transcendence

In his essay on metaphor, Derrida makes a distinction between how a philosopher and a theologian judge the status of metaphor. For the philosopher, he says, metaphor is a poor medium, always effacing the presence it seeks to illumine, subverting its own attempt at metaphysics by a "white mythology."[13] But he allows that "a theologian could be content with metaphor. And metaphor must be left to the theologian."[14] Good. I accept metaphor; it is all the theologian, I believe, needs. Metaphysical language—the language of certainty, of the absolute, claims to know God. But metaphor does not; it is modest. It makes a claim, but only with "assertorial lightness" or "soft focus," undercutting it immediately with the "is not."[15] The world is/is not the body of God. Both analogy and symbol make much bolder assertions: analogy rests on likeness between the cause and its effect (Thomas Aquinas), while symbols participate in the reality to which they point (Paul Tillich). But metaphor is more a heuristic fiction than a metaphysical claim. It invites us to imagine, to live "as if," to entertain a novel possibility, which initially both shocks and intrigues. The world is God's body? Surely not—and yet . . .

Metaphor is an "in-between strategy," avoiding the presumption of the *via positiva* and the silence of the *via negativa*. It respects deconstruction's fear of idolatry, essentialism, and fundamentalism but claims that this fear need not reduce us to silence or near silence. In

fact, it takes an entirely different strategy—piling on the language, going crazy like the psalmists and mystics do. It tells us to admit that our
language about God says little (if anything) about God, but rather than
exhibiting parsimonious humility that can scarcely mumble the word
"God," let us count on outrageous audacity to be its own negative, its
own critique. Two strategies are possible in order to underscore the
inadequacy, the nonsense, the falsity of God-talk. One advises us to
say little or nothing, secure in the knowledge that if we say nothing,
we will not be wrong. The other calls us to play with metaphors, many
metaphors, sucking the juice out of them and throwing them away (as
the Hebrew psalmists did), using everything and anything the world
provides for talking about God. Metaphorical theology avoids dead
metaphors that can pass as descriptions (God is king), preferring out-
landish suggestions (God is mother) that no one takes as literal. Nonetheless, even with its absurd metaphors (God as mother, the world as
God's body), it calls us to imagine ourselves *within* the world that these
shocking metaphors imply. Metaphor is a trickster, trying its chance,
seducing us to give it a chance, the chance of seeing *differently* and
maybe saying yes to a different way of being in the world.

As we dig more deeply into the potential of metaphor for
God-talk, let us dwell on the following comment by Merold Westphal:
"The critique of onto-theology . . . is directed not at *what* we say about
God but *how* we say it, to what purpose, in the service of what project?"[16]
He goes on to add, "We go to church in order to sing, and theology is
secondary."[17] If this is so, if language about God is mainly praise (and
not metaphysical assertions), then all sorts of language might be per-
missible—whatever language helps us to praise God more fully, more
appropriately. Would Derrida object to this use of metaphor? I think
not. What he does object to is metaphysics, which he defines as "concepts that have forgotten their metaphorical, sensuous base."[18] I object
to metaphysics also. Hegel believed that there was a hierarchy of images
and concepts, and we leave the former behind when we climb the ladder
of truth. This view claims that the concepts of metaphysics do not need
the concrete, sensuous base of metaphor; concepts rise above metaphor
and release themselves from their earthly, relative beginnings with their
built-in negation. But what if we did not forget the metaphoric base of
all God-talk? Suppose that what Hegel calls the language of children,
primitives, and women—the language of images—is the only language
we have to speak of God and that we stayed with it?[19] What if we also
always remember the "is not" of metaphor, so that it does not mutate

into symbol or analogy? What if we take as a watchword Derrida's claim that "metaphor . . . always has its own death within it"?[20] Were we to surround metaphor with these qualifications, could we then dare to let metaphor try its chance, be a detour between nonsense and truth, always aware that it can never be "true" and certainly not the truth, because it contains a "definite absence," its own death within it, the silent "is not" that is part of every metaphor?

It is necessary to underscore the difference between metaphor, symbol, and analogy (not to mention simile, allegory, story, and so on). Unlike these other forms of imagery, metaphor does not result in organic, systematic works. It does not stress the similarity, the participation, the secret wisdom, the narrative coherence, the sense of beginnings and endings, the relation between cause and effect that these others do. In fact, metaphor is closer to parable than to any of the above images.[21] It has the same disorienting shock and sense of novel recognition/insight as Jesus' parables. David Tracy suggests something similar when he says that the genre needed in our time is the metaphor of "fragment"— not narrative, analogy, or dialectic, but something similar to Kafka's fragmentary parables, which do not make the strong claim of symbols, but rather a slight one, "some hint of redemption, even if that redemption is neither understood . . . nor even fully experienced."[22] Metaphors are fragments, even the metaphors that become models, though well-established models of God—for instance, God as king or father—resist such designation. The world as God's body, a model with considerable explanatory potential for interpreting the God-world relationship, sin and salvation, and Christian discipleship, is also only a fragment.[23] Metaphors "say a lot"—good ones are rich with hermeneutical possibilities for making sense of things—but they do not "mean much." As Tracy writes, "If only Hegel had written the words 'A Thought Experiment' at the beginning of all his books, then Kafka would be the first, he says, to honor Hegel as the greatest of all philosophers. But of course Hegel did not."[24] Yet theologians are (or should be) content with metaphor, with thought experiments, as Derrida reminds us. This, I believe, is what all theology is; it never "advances" to a system, to metaphysics, to certain or absolute claims. It is always just metaphor.

After all, as Aristotle first set down, metaphor is saying something about one thing using language that belongs somewhere else. It is not, like symbol or other images, based on likeness, stressing similarity; rather, it takes all the richness, detail, and concreteness of things we know something about to try to give a glimmer of something we do not know much (if anything) about. Hence, "Love is a rose" can talk endlessly about roses—their smell, variety, texture, decay, and so forth—in order to hint about enigmatic "love." Likewise, "The world is God's body" gives us a great deal of language—the language of bodies, of earth, flesh, food, beauty, health, and sickness—as a way of speaking abut the transcendence and immanence of God, of divine presence. The world/body becomes a stand-in for what we do not know. Does all this rich language come to anything? Is it true? There is no way to know. Does this language help us to praise God? Yes, I think so. Does it also give direction as to how we should love our neighbors? Yes, I think it does. Metaphorical language is not principally about "truth"; rather, it is about gratitude for the gift of life and our attempts to show that gratitude.

The Sacramental and the Prophetic

We will shortly flesh out these two projects of metaphorical theology, but before leaving metaphors and models, let us put the issue of metaphorical language within the classic Christian dialectic of the sacramental and the prophetic. This is one of the oldest and most fruitful conversations. The sacramental sees continuity between God and the world; the prophetic, discontinuity.[25] The first has been characterized as the Catholic sensibility (Thomas Aquinas), the second as the Protestant sensibility (Karl Barth). The sacramental allows for the two books of revelation—nature and Scripture—while the prophetic insists on *sola scriptura*. The first sees the entire universe as the image of God, for nothing less could begin to reflect God's glory (Irenaeus, Augustine, Thomas Aquinas, G. M. Hopkins, Teilhard de Chardin); the second is terrified lest any visible, present thing claim to *be* the invisible presence of the divine. The first presses the iconic, advocating deification, the transparency of the world to its source, while the second fears idolatry, admonishing humility due to the opaqueness of all things before the wholly other. John Caputo suggests a similar dialectic with his notion of "historical association" and "messianic dissociation," the human need to concretize transcendence and the caution against doing so.[26] Another characterization is of course the kataphatic and the apophatic. These two impulses are both deep in the imagination of all religious traditions: the desire, indeed the need to speak of God, and the fear, the terror, of doing so.

Which is greater—the need or the fear—determines whether people veer toward one or the other extreme: fundamentalism (we have the truth in these words) or agnosticism (we have no truth in any words).

What I see as characteristic of the best of deconstruction's critique of theology is a desire to do something else: what Caputo calls "a happy minimalism."[27] This is excellent advice. It means that all of our versions, our interpretations, are always provisional and revisable: "Whatever was constructed in the first place is deconstructible."[28] This means, as he insists, that *we* must be responsible for our theologies; they are constructed, not given. We have only signs and traces, not the things themselves. I agree completely. He advises us (in good Thomistic fashion) to start "from below, *in medias res*, in the midst of the tumult, amidst supplements and signs, mediations and substitutes, without a heavenly hook to bail us out, doing the best we can. It is a question of beginning where one is, as Derrida tells us—not where God is, we may add."[29]

This makes eminent sense, except for Caputo's addition, "not where God is." Is there anywhere where God is not? Does the Thomistic rule of starting with the senses, with where we are, prohibit God from being here/there also? Augustine surely would say it does not, and so would the Jewish and Christian traditions that insist that God is Emmanuel, whether as the one who accompanied the Hebrews through their earthly trials or as the one who is incarnate in the flesh, in the world. The prophetic impulse does not negate the sacramental. And here we come to a crucial point: Need transcendence always mean what is *not* mundane? This seems to be an assumption, as suggested by Caputo when he speaks of determining "what is transcendent and what is mundane, what is original and what is copy, what is part and parcel of the calming reassurance and continuity of the same or immanence, and what belongs to the shock of the divine, the jolt and trauma of something different, of something—*grace a Dieu*—divine and discontinuous."[30] There appears to be a predilection in deconstruction, on the one hand, to privilege what cannot be said, the wholly other or *tout autre*, the prophetic silence, the sterile Protestant sensibility, the non-mundane, the invisible, as "transcendent." On the other hand, what is said, the sacramental, the words of praise, the fertile Catholic sensibility, the earthly and earthy, the historical and concrete—these are merely "immanent" and perhaps suspiciously idolatrous. Must, should, transcendence and immanence be seen as opposites? Is it not possible for there to be intimations of transcendence in our lowly, human practices of praise and compassion? I am, for example, intrigued by a comment by Simone Weil: "That God is good is a certainty. It is a definition. And it is even more certain that God—in some way that I do not understand—is reality."[31] The certainty and incomprehensibility that God is reality forms the background to the intimations of transcendence, praise and love, to which we now turn.

Living within the World as God's Body

We begin these reflections with a reminder of the earlier quotation by Simone Weil: "Humility is the only permitted form of self-love. Praise for God, compassion for creatures, humility for oneself."[32] Weil goes on to define humility as "attentive patience" and elsewhere writes that "attention animated by desire is the whole foundation of religious practices."[33] Paying attention is also at the center of a theology of the world as God's body. Weil says that we should look, not "eat." We seldom do this. Human love is usually "cannibalistic," wanting to use God and others for our own benefit, to fill up our own emptiness.[34] But the two distinctive intimations of transcendence we are considering— praising God and loving our neighbor—are characterized by an aesthetic distance, the ability to look but not devour, not possess. Love is the recognition of the other as other, whether God (the other as beauty) or our neighbor (the other as needy). The intimations of transcendence that come to us through the model of the world as God's body are ordinary—they arise from attentive patience to the actual, concrete, everyday world in which we live. To praise God through the glories of creation involves patient attention to small things—looking into the heart of a daffodil, hearing the splash of a frog in a pond, feeling the touch of another's hand. At certain times when we really pay attention to something outside ourselves—to the immensely complex beauty of the world—we want to repeat what God says in Genesis after creating the waters and the land, the sun and the moon, the plants and the animals, including human beings: "It is good. It is very good." God does not say that creation is good for himself or for human beings, but simply that it is good. To love our neighbor within the model of the world as God's body is also an ordinary everyday event. It involves attention to the needs, primarily the bodily, physical, mundane needs, of other human beings and other life-forms. It means feeding and clothing others;

trying to alleviate their pain and oppression; doing what is necessary so they may flourish. It involves, among other things, *knowing* what makes others flourish—"ecological literacy."

Discovering intimations of transcendence within the context of the world as God's body means being satisfied with *mediated* experiences of divine transcendence. "Back side" theology finds the glory of God in the beauty of the earth and in service to our neighbor. It means finding transcendence in the earth, in the flesh, in the ordinary, in the daily round. This is an odd suggestion, but one that I believe is at the heart of Christian faith, that "transcendence beyond transcendence" is radical immanence. Using the model of the world as God's body as a thought experiment for "transcendence beyond transcendence," we arrive at the place *where we are.* We meet God in and through the world, if we are ever to meet God. God is not out there or back there or yet to be, but hidden in the most ordinary things of our ordinary lives. If we cannot find the transcendent *in* the world, in its beauty and its suffering, then for us bodily, earthy creatures it is probably not to be found at all. Finding transcendence in and the through the earth means paying attention to others: the ethical rests on the aesthetic, the prior moment of realizing that something outside of oneself is real. Only then is one capable of the kenotic action, the retreat of one's relentless ego, to allow the glory of God and the need of the neighbor to fill oneself. The aesthetic is the recognition of otherness; the ethical is the practice of self-denial necessary so that others—God and neighbor—may be praised and served. Thus, with the thought experiment of the world as God's body, we can affirm with Simone Weil that "God is reality": the body of the world, the ordinary reality of our lives, is where we meet God. "God is reality": we find intimations of transcendence by rejoicing in the beauty of the real world and by serving the real needs of people and other life-forms. We conduct our ordinary lives within the divine milieu. All is divine, even this earth and its creatures, in ways we do not understand but of which we can become increasingly certain.

And how does one become certain? Not by thinking or even believing, but by living within the world *as if it were the body of God.* It involves the practice of paying attention to the world, to its beauty and its need. As the Catholic, sacramental sensibility has always insisted, this world is the only reality available to us and in and through it, we find God. Teilhard de Chardin expresses this sensibility when he says that from the time he was a child, he had two passions—a passion for the world and a passion for God—and he could not imagine giving up one for the other.[35] In this sensibility, visibility, and physicality are not shunned because of fear of idolatry; rather, as Francis Schüssler Fiorenza has said, "A theology that makes the fear of idols central may be a theology that ends up having room for neither icons of the divine nor the divine."[36] Or as Richard Kearney claims, "There is more to God than being. Granted. But to pass beyond being you have to pass through it."[37] And Weil notes, "How can Christianity call itself catholic if the universe itself is left out?"[38] Look and love, she says: look at the world and be astounded by its beauty: "Of all the attributes of God, only one is incarnated in the universe, in the body of the Word; it is beauty."[39] An incarnational theology gives us permission to love the body of the world and through the world's beauty to find intimations of God. An incarnational theology is suspicious of deconstruction's privileging of words over body, text over nature, interpretation over experience. While it is certainly not true that deconstruction claims "there is nothing outside the text" (as some simplistically believe), the physical world, both its beauty and its needs, is not often the focus of deconstruction. While we do indeed "construct" nature with our words, nature also constructs us with its beauty and its needs.[40] It confronts us with beauty that commands our attention (the "It is good" of Genesis). Nature also constructs us by confronting us with its inexorable and unavoidable laws and limits, its vulnerability and finitude, when faced with insatiable human greed. We too must eat—all of us—and no human construction of nature can erase nature's limitations as the one and only provider. Living within the model of the world as God's body awakens delight in each and every thing that makes up this body, but also an awareness of the needs of the body, its deprivations and sufferings.

What is this body that we are to praise and love? It is the universe, all matter/energy that has constituted physical reality since the Big Bang billions of years ago. It is not any one body and certainly not the human body (the model is not anthropomorphic or anthropocentric). The body of God is all of creation, all of nature, all that "is," all that exists. To imagine the world this way—as being in and of God—and to imagine God this way—as being the matrix of all that is—means that sharp lines between the world and God are erased.[41] The dualism of deism and theism is gone; we are in the realm of panentheism and perhaps pantheism. In order to underscore the immanence of God in the world, this model prefers to entertain the threat of pantheism in preference to the tradition's lapse into deism. Since our theologies will always be "wrong," is it better to err on the side of the presence or the absence of God? An incarnational theology opts for presence, with all of the caveats, qualifications, and negations that metaphor necessitates. This model, however, defends itself against pantheism with two subsidiary metaphors: first, as we are to our bodies, so God is to the world (the body infused, enlivened by mind/soul/spirit); and second, the world is in God as a baby is in the womb.[42] These metaphorical "fragments" by no means give us an organic system of the relations of God and the world. All they do is make some suggestions for thinking about the implications of the model.

Look and Love: Feeding the Body

I would prefer to dwell on the beauty of the world rather than its needs: most of us would. But they are related, as Dorothee Soelle suggests when she writes of those who side with the oppressed: "The resistance of Saint Francis or ... of Martin Luther King grew out of the perception of beauty. And the long lasting and most dangerous resistance is the one born of beauty."[43] We were created to desire God, to love God through the beauty of the earth. It is not fear that prompts us to pay attention to the world's needs, but delight and joy—Rilke's "Being here is magnificent." Indeed it is—agonizingly magnificent. Our daily thoughts of death are but the other side of our appreciation of the world's magnificence. We want simply to "be here" in the glory that we see in a child's smile, in fresh rain, or in the smell of an orange.

When Augustine's "God is love" is transposed into "Love is God," we are, says John Caputo, deflected away from knowing God and toward loving the neighbor, away from basking in the joy of simply being here toward doing something. "The *deflection* of God is the translation of God into a deed: Lord, when did we see You thirsty and give You to drink?"[44] Or as Edith Wyschogrod writes, "The saint's supreme *moral* principle is the *material* condition of the Other."[45] The intimation of transcendence at the heart of Christian faith is the awakening to the needs and sufferings of others. Loving God means feeding the suffering body of the world. Loving God is not a mystical immersion but a mundane task, a "female" nurturing, caring task. It is lowly and basic, having to do *first of all* with physical needs (food, water, housing) and physical pain (suffering, deterioration, destruction). Living within the model of the world as God's body means focusing on these material, bodily matters. It does not mean that there are no other needs (mental, spiritual, emotional, and so forth), but a metaphorical, incarnational theology privileges the lowly (and universal) physical needs. *All* must eat and *all* can suffer; hence, this model encourages us to find intimations of transcendence in and through the material conditions of others.

We prepare ourselves to do this by paying attention—by, as Weil puts it, looking, not eating: "The only people who have any hope of salvation are those who occasionally stop and look for a time, instead of eating."[46] Our tendency, says Weil, is to love others because of *our* needs, not theirs. Our fat, relentless egos want more, more, more; the insatiable greed of Adam Smith's economic man (*sic*) is but a contemporary version of original sin: the devouring, violent ego that wills to possess all. A first step in "salvation" is to stop and look and say with God, "It is good," and let it be. Educating the loving eye, the eye that pays attention to the other as other (in contrast to the arrogant eye that objectifies and uses others), involves a dispossession of the ego.[47] John Woolman, a remarkable eighteenth-century American Quaker and abolitionist, saw the connection between possessions and sin in slavery: an increasing desire for goods resulted in the oppression of others in order to meet that desire. "Every degree of luxury hath some connection with evil," he wrote.[48] To keep the self out of the center, the eye must be kept "single," that is, able to see the needs of others clearly. This singleness of sight can be achieved only by dispossessing the self of possessions. Otherwise, he claims we will always see double: the other will be seen only through the lens of the self's desires. At the close of his life, Woolman had a dream in which he heard a voice saying, "John Woolman is dead."[49] He interpreted this to mean the death of his own will; it meant that he was so mixed up with the mass of human beings that henceforth he could not consider himself a distinct being. His credo of universal love ended with his disappearance as a separate individual.

Likewise, Francis of Assisi's dispossession of the self in order to love others involved total poverty at both the material and the spiritual levels. Money and the ego, he believed, are the root of violence and exclusion; to live differently, one must dispose oneself of all possessions. Obedience is a kenotic movement, "a therapy for the liberation of desires," exemplified in the beggar archetype.[50] To be so liberated, one must give up not only money but authority, power, envy, self-glorification. One must become empty; in fact, one must become like a corpse: "This is true obedience: not to ask why you are moved, not to care where you are placed, not to insist on being somewhere else."[51]

This dispossession has been called many things: purification, conversion, purgation, repentance, de-creation. It is a process of kenosis, of self-emptying, that allows the other to be seen, that allows a place to be made for the other (not unlike divine kenosis in creation and incarnation, which "makes room" for creatures and the world). Self-limitation, sacrifice, asceticism, simplification: all of this language so typical of many religious traditions means nothing more than making space so others can be, can live. Furnishing this space is not easy. In fact, for people like us, who take up a lot of space—most of the space on the planet given our level of consumption—it is probably the hardest thing we can imagine. Can we empty ourselves of the self so that the other— the transcendent in the body of a hungry person or a clear-cut forest or an endangered species—might have room? Looking but not eating, kenosis, the single eye: these are not mere recommendations for our spiritual growth; rather, for us well-off North Americans, they are an intimation of transcendence—the command to let others live. Within the model of the world as God's body, this is as close to an absolute as one gets. Feed the body, not the self; look and love—do not devour.

An insatiable appetite is the mark of global market capitalism; it is also a definition of sin within the model of the world as God's body. "Salvation is consenting to die," writes Weil.[52] Excessive? Extreme? Not for us well-off human beings within a Christian incarnational context: if we pay attention to others, if their material condition becomes our central concern, we must decrease, retreat, and sacrifice so that others may be. Soelle writes, "Eventually the great majority of humankind hangs on the cross of empire and, in an extended mystical understanding of suffering, with her species and elements our mother earth, too, hangs on the cross of industrialism."[53] This statement implies that we meet God not face-to-face, but by way of God's "back side," the world, in its sickly, deteriorating, suffering condition. It is a prophetic cry to attend to a dimension of the divine, the world, that desperately needs our total attention and energies. As Wyschogrod puts it, "The term Other can be a collective sense as referring to the wretched of the earth." She goes on to say that "the saintly response to the Other entails putting his/her body and material goods at the disposal of the Other."[54] Wyschogrod calls this "carnal generality"—a disinterested saintly love expressed in one's entire corporeal being.[55] In other words, paying attention to other bodies (the material needs of others) demands doing so with one's own body (the material goods one possesses). Meeting God through the needs of other bodies by putting one's own body on the line: this is an intimation of transcendence as *radical immanence*. We meet God in and through other bodies, by laying down our own bodies for them. This theology of the cross is not a onetime atonement by God for humans; rather, it is a prophetic call for all to live differently *at the bodily level*. It is a call to attend first and foremost to the physical needs and health of planet Earth and its inhabitants. Body theology is basic theology: feed the hungry. Body theology is climate change theology: care for the planet.

But we do not want to hear this or see this. The model of the world as God's body is repulsive to us not because most of us are shocked by the linking of God and bodies (though some may be), but because we cannot imagine putting our own bodies and material goods at the disposal of the other. In a society where consumerism has become religion, where the insatiable individual is encouraged, the model is repugnant. It would mean looking at all the wretched of the earth—the teeming millions of the poor, the oppressed, the sick and dying—and making room for them. It would mean giving up some of our space, our place, our food so that others might eat and live. It is unimaginable to most of us. But its very offensiveness convinces me that it is perhaps an intimation of transcendence for our time and for people like us.

To focus on bodies, to dwell upon them, to pay attention to them: What might that bring about? Might it make us saints? Not likely, but it might mean a shift in our accepted anthropology, that is, in who we think we are in the scheme of things. It might make us realize that attending to the basic needs of creation's life-forms, human and non-human, is our job, our vocation, who we are in the scheme of things. Weil has a chilling passage in which a soul indicts God for allowing a hungry person to suffer: "Why have you forsaken him?" the soul asks. And in the silence that follows, the soul hears God's reply: "Why did *you* not feed him?"[56] This small anecdote contains the answer to the theodicy questions for the twenty-first century: God does not cause others to suffer; *we* do. One reason the world as God's body is an intimation of transcendence for us is that *we know this*. We know that much that has been blamed on God (the world's evils) are the result of our sin—our insatiable appetites that cause the growing gap between the rich and the poor and the deterioration of the planet. It is not God who does this; we do it. Therefore, the body, the material condition of bodies, the basics that all creatures need to live—this is our intimation of transcendence, our call from God: look and love; feed my world.

This chapter has been an exercise in minimalist Christian theology, theology limited to metaphorical statements and focused on the body of the earth in its glory as well as its horrifying deterioration. This exercise has suggested that a theology of praise and an ethic of compassion are needed elements for religious practice in a time of climate change. We have interpreted praise for the world and compassion for its vulnerability as intimations of transcendence, ways that postmodern Christians, who find presumptuous, absolutist statements about God unacceptable, can be religious in our time. Praise and compassion: praise deepens our wonder at and gratitude for the unimaginable beauty of our planet and the gift of living for a time on it; compassion emerges as our response to the loss of that beauty and gift—experienced now in climate change with a poignancy as never before. These two movements of transcendence—praise and compassion—are, I suggest, two actions desperately needed for the climate change sensibility. The more we love the earth, the more deeply we appreciate its wonders and glories, the readier we will be to sacrifice for it. One cares for what one loves, as parental love, among other kinds, illustrates. One does not need majestic mountains to gain this appreciation—a mundane occurrence such as learning that there are over eight hundred species of tarantulas will evoke awe in most of us!

Climate change will demand much of us. It will demand limits and sacrifices; it will demand that we *live differently*. Why should we do so? Not out of fear, duty, or necessity, but out of love. "The love of God is something to *do*"; namely, to praise God and have compassion for the world.[57] We stand with our feet firmly on the earth and exclaim, "I thank You God for most this amazing day,"[58] and then we get to work using our heads and hands, our imaginations and our money, our courage and our persistence to heal and restore our precious planet.

A Few Final Reflections

Let me close with a few personal comments. I know very little of what I am talking about. Sometimes I praise God through the beauty of the earth, and even fewer times do I try to renounce my ego and possessions so as to attend to the material condition of others. While both of these intimations of transcendence are only that—intimations—I believe, I trust, that they are so. I have found that my miserable attempts to live as if the world is God's body have brought about a few changes. I dare now to find God in the world (shocking for a former Barthian to admit), in and through everything in the world. I have become outrageously sacramental; I feel comfortable with language about God that is maternal, immanent, spirit-laden, oceanic, all-embracing. I feel as if I live within the divine milieu and can worship God in the intricacies, specialness, and particularity of each thing. I am not even afraid of pantheism; the line between God and the world is fuzzy.

As for the other, related intimation of transcendence—dispossessing myself that others might live—I have found it to be much harder. The most I can say is that I am certain it is true. I believe that is why we are here; it is who we are in the scheme of things—we are the agents, the mediators, who can work to help the rest of creation flourish. We are that part of the body of God that has become conscious of our proper role: to work with the incarnate God for the well-being of the earth. For us well-off human beings, however, the cost of doing this work will be enormous, as climate change is making very clear to us.

Finally, let us recall two important points about metaphors: many are needed, and they do not make large claims. The limits of the body model are obvious; no one model can function alone, lest it become hegemonic, become "descriptive," become the way things are. Erich Heller reminds us, "Be careful how you interpret the world. It *is* like that."[59] I have suggested that the body model is especially relevant as a way to interpret Christianity in our time of climate change, but other models are needed. Moreover, metaphors and models say a lot but mean little. The imaginative, as-if world they paint is rich and detailed, but the ontological assertion is slight. The "certainty" of metaphorical theology is not in its assertions but in the opportunity it provides to live differently. It allows "the world as God's body" to try its chance at serving as our way of being in the world. It is bold in filling out what life would be like within such a model, but modest in its claim of whether or not it is true. It is, at best, a faith, a hope, a possibility. Can people live committed, meaningful lives simply on faith and hope? But it may be enough. The gracious words of 1 Cor 13:13 tell us that faith, hope, and even love "abide," become our abode, our dwelling place, our home. We live here in and with God.

7

WHERE WE LIVE: URBAN ECOTHEOLOGY

Daily, our eating turns nature into culture, transforming the body of the world into our bodies and minds.
—Michael Pollan[1]

"Nature" is no longer "natural," nor do we know what we mean when we use the term. "Nature" used to be what one found in the country— animals, trees, mountains, and the sea—in contrast to what made up cities—people, buildings, cars, and culture. But now there is no un- touched "nature," no nature that has not been interpreted, constructed, or changed by human beings. The lines between nature and the human have become indistinct, fuzzy, confused. In addition, we postmoderns are so aware of our social constructions of nature that we no longer know how to speak of nature. Catherine Keller expresses this dilemma when she writes, "Indeed, in the effort to expose the human social con- structedness of the category Nature we do not yet have an adequate vocabulary for naming that reality that *is* us and is *more* than us, that *something* in which we are embedded and which remains, however we (re)construct it, irreducible to us."[2] Nature not only is "irreducible to us" but also is that upon which we rely every moment of our lives for air, water, food, and habitat. One of the consequences of our increasing awareness of human control over nature—both in thought and in action, in interpretation and in physical construction—*is the loss of a sense of our dependence on what is "more than us."* In our acknowledgment that there is no pristine nature, either in thought or in reality, we have lost the sense that we are products of, sustained by, and totally dependent on "nature"—whatever we call it and whatever it is. This forgetfulness is most evident in city dwellers, because cities are "second nature," what we have built from, transformed from, changed from "first nature," the "more than us" that is never reducible to us and our constructions.[3] Since city dwellers will soon compose more than half of the human population, this forgetfulness is a pressing problem, as global warming is warning us.

If the issues contained in the threat of climate change are to be addressed, we must overcome the forgetfulness of first nature. We must, as the city dwellers most of us now are, recall that nature is not just the trees, parks, and flowers in our cities, but rather it is the foundation of cities, the material from which cities are made. Every sidewalk, condo, office building, sewer pipe, electric grid, shopping mall, concert hall, parking lot, car and bus and train—*everything* in a city is made from nature. We do not see this nature that is the lifeblood of our cities since much of it is hidden in its new transformations—the trillions of energy exchanges that take place for every school, hospital, and jail that is built. Energy is used not only for transportation and electricity—when we drive our cars or light our houses and streets. *Everything we do that involves change of any sort takes place through an exchange of energy, and energy is nothing but first nature.* Therefore, we postmodern citizens of cities must acknowledge our situation: we are energy hogs in our use of first nature, even if we do not mean to be or are not even aware of it most of the time. *We must become aware of it.* This is the challenge that cities, prime examples of "second nature," pose to climate change.

The Nature of Nature

What *is* nature? Langdon Gilkey, theologian of nature, says nature has two meanings. "On the one hand, nature is represented in both archaic religion and modern science as the all-encompassing source or ground of all there is in concrete experience: the entities, inorganic and organic; the system of nature; ourselves; and even historical communities are products of nature."[4] In other words, there is nothing "outside" nature. But it is the second meaning Gilkey gives that raises the possibility of being outside nature: "Nature as a word, a concept, a symbol, signals on the other hand our distinction from, even our distance from, this environment."[5] In this second meaning, nature is "in part the construction of mind, the object of an active, intelligent, and purposeful subject."[6] This second meaning allows us to reduce what is the source of our being (nature in the first meaning) "to a level below us; to a means, to a system of objects to be examined, manipulated, and used; to a warehouse for goods needed by us."[7] Our ability to conceptualize "nature" is, of course, simply an example of what it means to be human: we human beings symbolize, interpret, reflect upon, conceptualize *everything*. It is the definition and distinctive activity of our species.

As geographer and student of cities Edward Soja points out, the product of human interpretation and manipulation does not erase nature; rather, it becomes a hybrid, as seen in urbanization. "The urban spatiality of Nature in essence 'denaturalizes' Nature and charges it with social meaning."[8] Soja adds, "Raw physical Nature may be naively or even divinely given to begin with, but once urban society comes into being, a new Nature is created that blends into and absorbs what existed before. One might say that the City *re-places* Nature."[9] Soja intends to undercut the conventional wisdom that views the natural and social worlds as separate, which he believes promotes dualism between nature and human beings. Rather, he suggests, we should focus on the hybrid—lived space—and especially on the city. When we privilege space and place, everything changes, he asserts. We no longer indulge in the binary dualism of nature versus culture, but realize that at least since the beginning of agriculture and hence of urbanization, nature has never been pristine. As Soja puts it, we have been "without nature" for twelve thousand years, which means, for all intents and purposes, always without it. There is no untouched nature, no wilderness—even Antarctica is "urbanized," that is, socially and historically constructed.

Highlighting space is a necessary corrective to the Western and Christian emphasis on time and history. It has several advantages. First, it focuses our attention on the earth (rather than on heaven) and does so by forcing us to attend to humanized space—cities—where most of us human beings now live. It spotlights the need for habitat, for humanely built spaces, here and now, rather than eternal places in heaven by-and-by. Second, it helps us to see that natural disasters are never only natural. It forces us to accept some responsibility for the effects of global warming as well as poverty. Third, it raises issues of power and privilege in ways that a naive focus on "first nature" fails to do; for instance, who lives in the big house on the hill, and who lives in the shack beside the railway tracks? Fourth, it prohibits the romantic notion that all we need to do is "get back to nature" as if nature were pure, good, and available as our guide in life.

This turn to space, especially urbanized space, suggests a revolution in Western thought as well as a timely attention to the space—cities— where climate change will meet its harshest test. The turn to space and place—focusing on the needs of billions of human bodies as well as trillions of other creatures—is recognition that we are not robots or cyborgs, but bodies that need space. Christianity's traditional concern with time and history and its relative indifference to space and place carries Gnostic overtones. We need to remind ourselves that "to be human . . . is to be placed."[10] As our planet becomes fuller with people and their increasing desire for high-energy lifestyles, *space* takes on new meaning. Everyone wants/needs more space as well as *a* place. Millions of displaced persons as well as cities of twelve to fifteen million human beings are the shadow side of the real estate selling motto "Location, location, location." Place, space, is about bodies and their most basic needs: food, water, habitat, medical care, education, work, and leisure. Time and history can bracket out these lowly bodily needs in order to focus on things of the mind and spirit: interpretation, meaning, and "eternal salvation."

Thus, a focus on cities is necessary. The *State of the World 2007* is subtitled *Our Urban Future.*[11] Within a few decades, the majority of the world's population will live in cities, which means that it is here that the most pressing issue of the twenty-first century—climate change—must be faced. The possibilities as well as the problems meet in cities: "Cities are now both pioneers of groundbreaking environmental policies and the direct or indirect source of most of the world's resource destruction and pollution."[12] On the one hand, "heavy reliance on fossil fuels, particularly in cities, is the primary driver of global climate change."[13] Cities need energy at every level: to erect buildings and infrastructure, to heat and cool buildings, to construct bridges and sidewalks, to transport people and goods, to light the streets, and even to create the parks that remind us of first nature. On the other hand, highly congested cities that build up rather than out are examples of energy conservation: "The dense environment of Manhattan more than compensates for its massive, often old and inefficient buildings, making New York City one of the most resource- and energy-efficient places in the United States."[14] Cities are not, then, the problem (in contrast, say, to rural or suburban living); in fact, in a "full planet" such as we now have, *good* cities will be part of the solution. As the *State of the World 2007* claims, "What will differentiate the good city [of the future] will be its capacity for reconciling its residents with nature. Socially just and environmentally sound cities—that is the quest!"[15]

But does this mean that "the City *re-places* Nature"? Soja speaks of "a new Nature" that "blends into and absorbs what existed before." This is, I think, exactly what we must not accept. I fear that such language, while appreciative of the hybrid, second nature of cities, allows for and in fact encourages us to forget first nature as the source of our being. Jane Jacobs said that "without cities, we would be poor," but I would add that "without nature, we would not exist."[16] If we think of the city as absorbing or replacing nature, I fear that nature's intrinsic value as well as its finite limits will be hidden from our view. What, then, will deter our appetite for unlimited, voracious overutilization of other life-forms and earth processes? The Earth Charter lists as its first principle: "Respect Earth and life in all its diversity. Recognize that all beings are interdependent and every form of life has value regardless of its worth to human beings."[17] The hybrid model of city as nature tends to hide the "rights" of other life-forms as well as our necessary care for these others on whom we depend absolutely.

Nature Encompasses the City

While the city in many ways has replaced nature, both concretely as the habitat of most human beings and as our own construction, the bottom line is that we are totally and continually dependent on nature and its services. Nature in the first sense—"the all-encompassing source or ground of all there is"—and more specifically our own planet Earth with its particular constitution of elements suitable for living things, is the sine qua non. No matter how much we transform first nature, as epitomized by the city and by our myriad interpretations, it is not infinitely malleable. Global warming is one very powerful argument supporting this statement. In the space of a few hundred years of excessive use of fossil fuels, we human beings have managed to bring the planet to the brink of climate change so profound that many scientists now fear we will soon reach the tipping point of an uncontrollable, exponential rise in world temperatures. Our transformation of first nature, when we lived as hunter-gatherers, into second nature—the hybridization of the twenty-first-century city—now faces us with the deterioration and destruction of everything we hold dear. The human ability to distance ourselves from first nature, both by changing it and by objectifying it, is causing a deep forgetfulness to overtake us.

This forgetfulness is epitomized in the city dweller's relationship to food. Our ability to distance ourselves from first nature is nowhere more evident than in our ignorance and denial of our total dependence on the earth with every mouthful we eat. As Michael Pollan puts it in his book tracing "the natural history of four meals," "All flesh is grass." The scriptural text takes on new meaning when we consider that even a Twinkie or a Big Mac "begins with a particular plant growing in a specific patch of soil . . . somewhere on earth."[18] Our flesh (and the flesh that we eat) can be traced back to the grass that feeds us. "At either end of any food chain you find a biological system—a patch of soil, a human body—and the health of one is converted—literally—to the health of the other."[19] And yet we city dwellers have forgotten this all-important piece of information: the inexorable, undeniable link between our health and the health of the planet. The physicality of the connection needs to be underscored: it is from body to body. "Daily, our eating turns nature into culture, transforming *the body of the world into our bodies and minds*" (emphasis added).[20] It is impossible to make our absolute dependence on first nature any clearer. We need to relearn the importance of this most basic of all transformations. "For we would [then] no longer need any reminder that however we choose to feed ourselves, we eat by the grace of nature, not industry, and what we're eating is never anything more or less than *the body of the world*" (emphasis added).[21]

But urban dwellers seldom see this. The city is the prime example of both our greatest accomplishment and our greatest danger. Jerusalem, the city of desire and delight, is fast emerging as Babylon, the city of excessive luxury in the midst of extreme poverty. The city, which stands as the quintessential human habitation—civilized, diverse, cosmopolitan—is at the same time becoming the greatest threat to human well-being. "Of all the recognized ecological systems it is human urbanism which seems most destructive of its host."[22] Cities suck energy from near and far to allow some city dwellers to live at the highest level of comfort and convenience ever known, while many others exist in squalor. Cities of twelve million or more are divided, to be sure by class, race, and gender, but also by the space they occupy and the energy they can command. A spacious condo overlooking the harbor, with all of the electronic devices desired, is the sign of the successful city dweller. But having transformed first nature so thoroughly into the built, utilized environment, we are no longer aware of nature as source, as that which feeds us every mouthful we eat and provides us with every breath we take. We can forget first nature.

But *can* we? Botanist and conservationist Peter Raven summarizes our impact on the biosphere as follows: "Overall the condition can only be described as unsustainable, which means that we are changing the world and using its resources much more rapidly than they can be renewed, and leaving for our children and grandchildren a world that will be much less diverse, rich, healthy, and resilient than the one in which we live now."[23] This appears as well to be the judgment of the United Nations Millennium Ecosystem Assessment (MA), the work of more than thirteen hundred experts worldwide and "the first attempt by the scientific community to describe and evaluate on a global scale the full range of services people desire from nature."[24] The sobering conclusion of this massive study is that out of twenty-four essential services that nature provides for humanity, nearly two-thirds are in decline. These services are all-encompassing, falling into three major categories: provisioning services (food, fiber, genetic resources, biochemicals and natural medicines, fresh water); regulating services (air, climate, water, erosion, disease, pest, pollination, natural hazard); and cultural services (spiritual and religious values, aesthetic values, recreation, ecotourism).[25] As the MA puts it, "In effect, the benefits reaped from our engineering of the planet have been achieved by running down natural capital assets." [26]

Yet nature's services are seldom appreciated; they are often hidden, particularly from city dwellers, for whom clean water comes from the faucet and food from the supermarket. First nature provides these services "free" to the planet's inhabitants, but as the MA points out, as societies become more complex and technologically advanced, it is "easy to gain the impression that we no longer depend on natural systems."[27] The first sentence of the MA attempts to correct this misconception: "Everyone in the world depends on nature and ecosystem services to provide the conditions for a decent, healthy, and secure life."[28] Needless to say, however, these necessary services are not shared equally. The difference between the rich and the poor on our planet can be measured by the availability or nonavailability of nature's services. Wealthy individuals benefit from an excess of food, clean water, freedom from disease, climate regulation, and so on, while poor people suffer from a lack of these things. It is not money that separates the rich and the poor so much as it is the availability of basic services. In societies where food, housing, and medical care are available to all, regardless of the ability to pay, the gap between the rich and the poor is less pronounced and less painful.

Hence, the importance of the just distribution of nature's services as well as their sustainability cannot be overstated. The MA stresses the need for consciousness-raising: "We must learn to recognize the true value of nature both in an economic sense and in the richness it provides to our lives in ways more difficult to put numbers on."[29] Such true value ranges from the taste of a cup of clean water to the sight of snowcapped mountains. We are nature's debtors and nature's lovers. Anthropologist David Harvey sums up the situation well with these sobering words:

> A strong case can be made that the humanly-induced environmental transformations now under way are larger scale, riskier, and more far reaching and complex in their implications (materially, spiritually, aesthetically) than ever before in human history. The quantitative shifts that have occurred in the last half of the twentieth century . . . imply a qualitative shift in environmental impacts and potential unintended consequences that requires a comparable qualitative shift in our responses and our thinking.[30]

Thinking Differently

The task before us—"a qualitative shift in our responses and our thinking"—is daunting. Yet such appears to be the overwhelming conclusion coming from all fields that study planetary health. As Raven says, "It is also a fundamentally spiritual task."[31] After stating what geography, anthropology, biology, and sociology can contribute to the planetary crisis, most scholars agree that an attitude change is needed as well, a shift in values at a deep level. From the time of Aristotle to the eighteenth century, economics was considered a subdivision of ethics: the good life was understood to be based on such values as the common good, justice, and limits. Having lost this context for how to live on our planet and substituting the insatiable greed of market capitalism in its stead, we are now without the means to make the qualitative shift in thinking that is required. With the death of communism and the decline of socialism, Western society is left with an image of human life that is radically individualistic. This view is diametrically opposed to the way we should think of ourselves within an ecological worldview. It is impossible to imagine us acting differently—acting as "ecological citizens"—unless we internalize ecological values.[32]

One of the distinctive activities of religion is the formation of basic assumptions regarding human nature and our place in the scheme of things. As theologians widely agree, all theology is anthropology. Religious traditions educate through stories, images, and metaphors, creating in their adherents deep and often unconscious assumptions about who human beings are and how they should act. Religions are in the business of forming the imagination and thus influencing the actions of people. It is at this point that the religions can make a significant contribution to the planetary crisis. For we live *within* the assumptions, the constructions, of who we think we are. As these assumptions, constructions, change, so might behavior. One small contribution toward this possibility is to change the metaphor by which we think of ourselves in the world. The metaphor that is conventional and widely accepted in twenty-first-century market capitalism is *the individual in the machine*. Human beings are seen as subjects in an objectified world that is there for our use—our needs, desires, and recreation. The world is a "thing" to be utilized for human needs and pleasure. This view of ourselves, however, is an anomaly in human history, for until the scientific revolution of the seventeenth century, as Carolyn Merchant and others have pointed out, the earth was assumed to be alive, even as we are.[33] From the Stoics to the medieval Christians to Indigenous Peoples, the apparent organic quality of the earth was not questioned. But during the last few hundred years, it has become increasingly useful and profitable to think of the world more like a machine than a body. Since we always think in metaphors—especially at the deepest level of our worldviews—the nature of the metaphor becomes critical. If the machine model is dominant, then we will think of the world's parts as only externally related, able to be repaired like cars, with new parts substituting for faulty ones, with few consequences for the earth as a whole. With such a basic model in mind, it is hard for people to see the tragedy of clear-cut forest practices or the implications of global warming.

The "individual in the machine" model fits easily into the sensibility of city dwellers. Since most of us have a difficult time recognizing first nature as the source of the buildings, trucks, machines, and highways we construct, thinking of the world in terms of exchangeable parts is easy. Cities do not appear to be organic entities made from the earth; rather, they have independent parts "made by human beings" that can be torn down when needed and new ones constructed. However, the "body" is reemerging across many fields of study as a basic metaphor for interpretation and action. David Harvey mentions "the extraordinary efflorescence of interest in 'the body' as a grounding for all sorts of theoretical enquiries over the last two decades or so."[34] As we have noted, this interest is hardly novel: from the Socratic notion of the body ("man") as the measure of all things to the Stoic metaphor of the world as a living organism and Indigenous Peoples' understanding of the earth as "mother" of us all, body language has historically been central to the interpretation of our place in the scheme of things. This is true of Christianity as well. As an incarnational religion, Christianity has focused on bodily metaphors: Jesus as the incarnate God, the Eucharist as the body and blood of Christ, the church as the body of Christ.[35] The view that sees bodily well-being as the measure of both human and planetary well-being is so obvious that it seems strange that it should need a revival. What is gradually surfacing once again is the realization that an appropriate metaphor with which to imagine our relation to the world is not *the individual in the machine*, but *bodies living with the body of the earth*. And this is as true of city dwellers as it is of country folks. City dwellers need to "think differently," to think of their place—the city—as made from nature, from countless energy exchanges, all of which add greenhouse gases to the atmosphere. However, behind the twenty-first-century destruction of the planet and the impoverishment of the majority of its inhabitants lies a very different assumption about human beings: we are individuals with external relations to one another and to the planet itself.

Before proceeding further with the body model (or any other model), we must note that all metaphors are partial, none are adequate, and all need supplementation from other metaphors.[36] Metaphors are not descriptions; rather, they are the principal epistemological tool available to us for considering matters having to do with our most basic assumptions about ourselves and our world. We judge metaphors not by descriptive agreement, but by a shock of recognition that follows initial disbelief. Thus, as Jacques Derrida points out, metaphor lies somewhere between nonsense and truth, and we entertain the nonsense for a while to see if it contains any truth.[37] So imagining the world as a body engenders an initial suspicion followed by an acknowledgment of possibility—and eventually, if the metaphor turns out to be an enduring model, by acceptance and familiarity. In addition, however, to this set of criteria for a good model, one other factor is crucial: What are the results of living within it? What does thinking within this model do to our acting within it?

We have seen the results of living within the machine model for several hundred years now, and the verdict is overwhelmingly negative. Is it time to return to the model of the world—and ourselves—as body? The body as measure, as the lens through which we view the world and ourselves, changes everything. It means that human beings as bodies, dependent on other bodies and on the body of the earth, are interrelated and interdependent in infinite mind-boggling, wonderful, and risky ways. It means that *materialism*, in the sense of what makes for bodily well-being for all humans and for the earth, becomes the measure of the good life. It combines the socialist with the ecological vision of human and planetary flourishing. It means that the good life cannot be the hoarding by a few individuals of basic resources for their own comfort and enjoyment. Rather, if we desire to take care of ourselves, we also must take care of the world, for we are, in this metaphor, internally related and mutually dependent on all other parts of the body. The metaphor of body—not just the human body but all bodies (all matter)—is a radically egalitarian measure of the good life: it claims that all deserve the *basics* (food, habitat, clean air and water, and so forth).

This model turns our thinking upside down, for it makes two claims at odds with the mechanistic model. First, it claims that we human beings can no longer see ourselves as controlling all of the other "parts"; rather, we must acknowledge that as the creature at the top of the food chain, we are totally dependent on all of the others who are presumably "beneath us." Second, it impels us to acknowledge that the 20 percent of us who use 80 percent of the world's energy are responsible for the crushing poverty on our planet through our refusal to share resources equitably among all human beings and other creatures. In other words, this model helps us to see that sustainability and just distribution of resources are but two sides of the same coin: in order for the earth to be healthy long-term, the basic resources of life must be shared equitably among all creatures.[38] In other words, the individualistic, greedy assumptions of market capitalism are false: human beings cannot flourish apart from the flourishing of all the constituents that make up the earth. The earth is more like a body than a machine. Returning to the wisdom of our forebears and living within the body model rather than within the machine appears to be an appropriate move.

This move, I believe, will help us in our central political task as expressed by Harvey: "Suffice it to say that the integration of the urbanization question into the environmental-ecological question is a sine qua non for the twenty-first century."[39] The urbanization and the ecological questions meet in the city: "A city can be thought of as a mechanism to provide its inhabitants with ecosystem services."[40] Thinking of ourselves as bodies, our world as a body, and our cities as delivering nature's services to bodies may be a helpful imaginative exercise after centuries of mechanistic, individualistic metaphors. If we were to think of ourselves, our world, and our cities through the organic metaphor, what difference might it make in our behavior, and specifically, what help might it give us to face the realities of climate change?

Christianity and the Body Metaphor

I would like now to investigate in more detail the contribution of a Christian understanding of the organic model for twenty-first-century urban living. The Christian incarnational understanding of the God-world relationship—that the world is from the beginning loved by God and is a reflection of the divine—means that flesh, bodies, space and place, air and water, food and habitat are all "religious" matters. The locus of attention of incarnational Christianity is *the body*, both the world as body and the bodies that compose it. The *material* focus becomes central; incarnational theology is militantly anti-Gnostic, anti-spiritualizing, anti-dualistic. The Christian incarnational focus on bodies can be seen in the two central historical streams in Christianity: the sacramental and the prophetic, or the Catholic and the Protestant. The sacramental stresses continuity between the world and God—the world is a sacrament of God—while the prophetic underscores distance between God and the world. The sacramental dimension says that the world is a reflection of God, tells us of God, and connects the earthly, bodily joys of life (beauty, love, food, music, play) with God. The prophetic dimension insists that since the world is a body, it must be fed and cared for: all parts must receive their just supply of resources, and the earth must be sustained for the indefinite future.

The Sacramental Dimension

Those living within the model of the world as God's body see the world differently: not as an object or a machine or simply a resource, but as sacred, valuable, and needing our care. The world, including nature, is not ours to do with as we wish. It all belongs to and tells us of God. The sacramental dimension claims that nature is an image of the divine; it is a reflection of God in all of God's diverse beauty.[41] Hence, while the sacramental dimension of the model connects us to God, it does so only through the millions of different bodies that make up the world. It suggests a celebration of bodies as well as a concern for the care and feeding of bodies that underscores our respect for their intrinsic worth as part of God's creation.

The sacramental dimension of the model of the world as God's body prohibits us from folding first nature into second nature, since it suggests that nature, ours and everything else, does not belong to us in the first place. It is "other." The interpretation of nature as sacrament of God demands a different stance, one suggested by Henry David Thoreau's comment that "wildness" was in the second-growth forest at Walden Pond in Concord. "Wildness" is in the mind as well as in reality; it is our recognition of otherness. In the words of philosopher Iris Murdoch, "Love is the extremely difficult realization that something other than oneself is real. Love . . . is the discovery of reality."[42] In other words, love is not a sentimental emotion or an act of charity; rather, it is the objective recognition that others exist, have intrinsic worth, and have rights to the basics of existence.

This sense of the "other" is evident also in the story of creation in Genesis. While Christianity has often been condemned as a chief contributor to environmental destruction with its slogan from Genesis, "Subdue and dominate," we should also note a very different sensibility within that text. After each creation—of the light and darkness, the waters and the land, the sun and the moon, all fish in the sea and birds in the air and animals on the land—including human beings—God says, "It is good." God then gave to every beast and bird and other living creature the green plants to share among themselves. Having created all things and given them food for flourishing, "God saw everything that he had made, and indeed, it was very good" (Gen 1:31). Two points stand out in this story: God says of creation, "It is good," not good for human beings (or even for the divine self!), but simply "good." This is an aesthetic statement of the intrinsic worth of each and every creature, echoing the first principle of the Earth Charter. Second, the green plants are given to *all* living creatures to share. In sum, God says of creation, "It is good," seven times, but God says to "subdue and dominate" just once—and that within the context of the just distribution of plants to all creatures. This story supports both the intrinsic worth of others and their right to the basics of existence.

Thus, a sacramental understanding of the world suggests a sensibility that appreciates the world in its beauty and value; sees the world as a reflection of God; and comprehends that the world is a body made up of bodies, and thus all parts must be fed and cared for. Such a sensibility cannot imagine replacing the world with human interpretations and constructions. A sacramental sensibility supports the "irreducibility" of nature, its "more than us" quality, its "otherness" as belonging to God, not to us. It suggests that the Christian response is gratitude for the wonder of the world and recognition of our total dependence on it. Such an attitude toward the world can acknowledge that human beings have indeed constructed the world in which we live; that there is no uninterpreted, pristine, or untouched nature left. Nonetheless, it is still possible to hold, if one lives within this model, that a sensibility of appreciation of and care for "others" is an imperative—and that it is a realistic assessment as well.

The Prophetic Dimension

While the sacramental dimension of the model of creation as God's body encourages us to appreciate and love others—to realize their worth—the prophetic dimension focuses our attention on limits—the recognition that bodies, including the body of the world, are finite. All life-forms must have food, fresh water, clean air, and a habitat. The prophetic dimension stresses the limits of all bodies, the finitude of the planet, the need for just and sustainable use of resources. More specifically, within the built environment, the twelve thousand years of gradual urbanization, the organic model of the world places severe limits on the excess, hoarding, greed, and injustice of some parts of the body—namely, the well-off 20 percent of human beings who are contributing to the destruction of the planet and the impoverishment of fellow human beings.

The central issue at the Third Session of the World Urban Forum that met in June 2006 in Vancouver was the projection by the UN's latest evaluation of cities that slum living is now among the fastest-growing legacies of "civilization."[43] Given present trends, one out of three city dwellers will be doomed to the slums. The conditions in many cities—those pushing fifteen million—are already dire. The needs resulting from the doubling of city populations by mid-century from the present two billion to four billion are mind-boggling.[44] Housing, public health, transportation, energy, food and water, education, and medical services are simply the basics for minimal human existence. The forum met in a city—Vancouver—widely praised as one of the most livable and well built in the world; it epitomizes the "compact" city with its high-density population core of business and residential buildings, good public transit, numerous parks, and the greatest percentage of pedestrians and cyclists of any North American city. It is a dream city. But even Vancouver has the Downtown Eastside, an area of great poverty and drug addiction, an indication of things to come in the cities of the future, according to the forum. Vancouver is an example of the two sides of cities—the New Jerusalem and Babylon—with the latter projected as humanity's destiny.

Is the organic model relevant to the upcoming urban crisis? The prophetic dimension of the model—the awareness of the finitude, limits, and needs of bodies—suggests that it is. In fact, this dimension must take center stage. *Our very survival may well rest on living within such a construction of nature—one in which "second nature" is constrained.* The prophetic dimension of the organic model, which sees all bodies as needing the basics, suggests a "kenotic sensibility" for twenty-first-century well-off urban dwellers, so that the projected slum dwellers may have space and place.

Kenosis means to empty, to pull back, to limit. The term is traditional in Christian theology as a way to understand both God's creation of the world and the incarnation in Jesus Christ. In creation, God allowed space for others to exist by divine limitation, not as a self-denying act but as an affirmation of the other, in a way similar to the Genesis announcement, "It is good." In the incarnation, according to Pauline text, Christ, "though he was in the form of God, did not regard equality with God as something to be exploited, but emptied himself, taking the form of a slave, being born in human likeness" (Phil 2:6-7).[45] Kenosis is a unifying theme in Christian thought, extending beyond God's actions in creation and the incarnation to include the discipleship of followers. As Paul reminds his flock, "Let each of you look not to your own interests, but to the interests of others. Let the same mind be in you that was in Christ Jesus" (Phil 2:4); namely, follow the self-emptying Christ. *Kenosis—self-limitation so that others may have place and space to grow and flourish—is the way God acts toward the world and the way people should act toward one another and toward creation.* The notion of self-limitation for the well-being of others is widespread among many religions, as evident in the emptying God in Buddhism and in Gandhi's notions of *ahimsa* (reverence for all living things) and *satyagraha* (soul or love force).[46] In both Buddhism and Christianity, compassion toward others is based on self-emptying, which, paradoxically, is also the way to true fullness: those who would save their lives must lose them.

At the heart of kenotic thinking is the assumption that bodies need space. As benign as this idea might sound, it is one plausible description of sainthood. Edith Wyschogrod, in her book *Saints and Postmodernism*, writes, "The term Other can be given a collective sense referring to the wretched of the earth." She goes on to say that "the saintly response to the Other entails putting his/her body and material goods at the disposal of the Other."[47] In other words, attention to others means attention to bodies, to the material needs of others, and paying attention to other bodies demands doing so with one's own body (the material goods one possesses). For well-off people, who take up most of the space on the planet (having a huge "ecological footprint"), the prophetic, kenotic dimension of the organic world model is painful. It means pulling back, limiting oneself, learning to distinguish between needs and desires, saying one has "enough," being willing to sacrifice for the common good. The new epistemological turn from time and history to space and place means for Christians, at least, the end of supposing that salvation is concerned with souls in heaven; now it is clearly acknowledged to refer to bodies on earth. For the fortunate 20 percent, it means emptying the self of its insatiable appetites so that others have the space for habitat, for food, for life itself.

The turn to the organic model as a way of imagining the world—and ourselves in the world—suggests both a personal and a planetary economic practice. In Christianity as well as many other religions, the diminishment of the ego is often seen as central to spiritual maturity. Emptying oneself that God may enter, may become the center of the self, is understood as the way to fulfillment. What is widespread in religions as a personal practice—taking up less "ego space"—is reflected at the planetary level as the demand that we diminish our ecological footprint. Spiritual space and bodily space are related: those with insatiable ego-gratifying desires use up huge amounts of physical space with their rampant consumption, large energy-hungry dwellings, and jet travel lifestyles. Ego and eco—soul and body—are mysteriously related both at the level of our personal lives and at the level of planetary health. To be "saved," to "find one's life," to be fulfilled, appears to be a practice of mental and bodily limitation, diminishment, so that space may be given to others—to God and other people and other life-forms. Simone Weil's notion of "decreation" involved diminishing her own ego so that God might grow in her, and she might become a channel of God's love to others.[48] But through the experience of near starvation in France during World War II, she also saw the necessity of "decreating" at the bodily level: she disciplined herself to eat no more than her neediest neighbors. Her example is an illuminating concrete illustration of what we now see we must do: limit our "wants" to "needs," shrink our swollen Western egos and sense of entitlement in order that others might have space to live. The saintly admonition to lose one's life both at the level of the ego and at the bodily level appears to hold a suggestion also for just, sustainable planetary living: kenoticism is not the denial of life but the way to fulfillment of life for all. What begins as a personal, spiritual practice—self-limitation in terms of ego and material needs—can and should become an ethic for global health. Ego is a space issue, and so is planetary economics—is this a plausible and illuminating connection?

For well-off city dwellers, the prophetic, kenotic sensibility means some concrete, empirical, on-the-ground changes. It means that second nature, the built environment, must be minimized rather than maximized. It means small condos and apartments, not mansions; living spaces that go up, not out; small, hybrid cars, not Hummers; food that is grown locally, not halfway around the world. It means saying no, saying, "Enough!" Second nature is built upon first nature, and first nature is, increasingly, a vulnerable, deteriorating body unable to support the Western high-energy lifestyle. This realization should impact us at all levels: the food we eat, our means of transportation, the clothes we wear, the places we live, the parks where we play, the offices where we work. One of the greatest challenges of the twenty-first century is the provision of decent, livable conditions for the billions who will live in cities. We well-off city dwellers need to take up less space, use less energy, lower our desire for more, attend to needs before wants—become small, in other words. The prophetic, kenotic sensibility demands that prosperous urban dwellers retreat from expansion and accept simplification at all levels of existence. Justice and sustainability demand that whatever we build upon first nature be shared with all other beings and be done within the limits of the planet's resources.

In sum, second nature needs to acknowledge the base on which it is built and on which it will continue to depend—first nature. Totalizing theories that eliminate first nature forget that we are *bodies* before all else. *We cannot interpret or build unless we can eat.* While we are also and at the same time interpreters and builders of our world, we are not its maker or master. There is something outside all of our interpretations and constructions: the air we must breathe, the water we must drink, and the food we must eat. An understanding of second nature that underestimates the inescapable importance of first nature is not only unhelpful in our planetary crisis, but also false. It does not help us to live the best we can, making decisions that are relatively better, even if Eden—first nature—is no longer available. An organic model of the world reminds us of the sacredness, beauty, and importance of first nature at both the local and the planetary levels. It reminds us there is a difference between a small city lot that is zoned for a pocket park and one that is tarred over for cars. It reminds us also that our planet is a limited physical entity able to support millions of species including human beings, but only on a just and sustainable basis.

The kenotic God who opened up space for creation and who became empty in the incarnation is far removed from the image of an absolute, unmoved ruler who controls others by demanding total obedience. The power of the kenotic God lies in giving space for others, dying to self that others might live. This strange reversal—losing one's life to save it—is also the sensibility that is needed if our planet is to survive and prosper. Giving space is a basic Christian doctrine, but it is also deep at the center of most religions—and it is felt in the hearts of all people, religious or not, who know that "love is the discovery of reality," the realization that something beside oneself is real. Other bodies exist and must be fed and cared for. Once that acknowledgment is internalized, there is no going back to the assumption that individuals can pursue their own good apart from the good of others.

The organic model of the world is a fit one for twenty-first-century urban life: it suggests a context, a way of thinking, a construction within which to live, that underscores the beauty and intrinsic value of what is left of first nature as well as our inexorable dependence on it. It helps to situate human beings in an appropriate stance toward the world: a stance of gratitude and care, gratitude for the wonder of living on this beautiful planet (as the poet Rilke puts it, "Being here is magnificent"), and care for its fragile, deteriorating creatures and systems. We do not own the earth—we do not even pay rent for it; it is given to us "free" for our lifetime, with the proviso that we treat it with the honor it deserves: appreciating it as a reflection of the divine and loving it as our mother and our neighbor.

PART FOUR

Despair and
Hope within
Climate Change

8

IS a DIFFERENT WORLD POSSIBLE? HUMAN DIGNITY and the INTEGRITY of CREATION

For I am about to create new heavens
*   and a new earth;*
the former things shall not be remembered
*   or come to mind.*
But be glad and rejoice forever
*   in what I am creating:*
for I am about to create Jerusalem as a joy,
*   and its people as a delight. . . .*
No more shall the sound of weeping be heard in it,
*   or the cry of distress.*
No more shall there be in it
*   an infant that lives but a few days,*
*   or an old person who does not live out a lifetime. . . .*
For like the days of a tree shall the days of my people be,
*   and my chosen shall long enjoy the work of their hands.*
They shall not labor in vain,
*   or bear children for calamity;*
for they shall be offspring blessed by the LORD. *. . .*
Before they call I will answer,
*   while they are yet speaking I will hear.*
The wolf and the lamb shall feed together,
*   the lion shall eat straw like the ox. . . .*

They shall not hurt or destroy
on all my holy mountain,
says the LORD.
—Isa 65:17-25

Reading this passage makes us weep—weep for our world, our poor, sorry world. The world we want, that we ache for, is a world where children get to grow up and live to old age, where people have food and houses and enjoyable work, where animals and plants and human beings live together on the earth in harmony, where none "shall hurt or destroy." This is our dream, our deepest desire, the image we cannot let go of. This vision of the good life makes us unwilling to settle for the unjust, unsustainable, and indeed cruel and horrendous world we have. Global warming seems like the last straw: "Things are not supposed to be this way. A different world is possible." Isaiah's hymn to a new creation and Jesus' parables of the reign of God touch this deepest desire in each of us for a different, better world. It would be a world in which human dignity and the integrity of creation are central, a world in which the intrinsic value of all human beings and of the creation itself is recognized and appreciated. Human dignity and the integrity of creation lie at the heart of the biblical vision of the good life, and at the heart of our contemporary vision as well. Do we have any hope for a different, better world? Given the situation we face at the beginning of the twenty-first century of war, violence, AIDS, capitalist greed, and now the specter of global warming, it seems absurd to even bother with such a question. And yet we read in the Isaiah passage that in the midst of painting this wonderful picture of life beyond our wildest dreams, God says, "Before they call I will answer, while they are yet speaking I will hear." *"While they are yet speaking"*—we have only to ask for God to answer! But we must ask with our whole being; a better world must become our deepest desire. And this means, of course, we must *work at it*; we must give our whole selves to it.

First, let us look at the kind of destruction that our world is presently undergoing—this will be an analysis of what is wrong. Then we will consider what we need to do to turn things around; in other words, our preliminary work so that God may answer.

Since September 11, 2001, terrorism appears to many people as the major kind of destruction we face. Terrorist acts are sharp, clear, and horrible: we all react instinctively to them with fear and loathing. Terrorist acts encourage us to see ourselves as good and the destroyers as evil; they provide us with an enemy for our world's troubles that is not ourselves. Of course, when we dig deeper and look at the roots of terrorism—things such as poverty, racism, market greed, the struggle for arable land and clean water—a whole different picture emerges of who is to blame. But our current popular analysis of acts of terror does not encourage this kind of thinking. Rather, it tells us that the terrorists are evil and that we, on the other hand, are basically good, or at least okay.

But there is another kind of destruction that is slower, deeper, and involves us more clearly, epitomized by climate change. Here it is more difficult to escape the root analysis that, as with terrorism, we are somehow involved—our understanding of who we are and how we should be acting is part of the world we see before us. More people, including children, die in a world being destroyed by climate change than from terrorist acts; the dying is slower and for the most part out of our sight. As such, it allows for our denial and indifference; in other words, for sins of omission. Unlike terrorists, we don't actually have to commit evil acts to participate in the evil of climate change: our very existence as well-off North Americans living the good consumer life assures that we are involved. Even when we try to hide our heads, saying that we don't yet have all the facts about climate change, we know we are rationalizing. We know we would rather focus on the terrorists and their blatant evil acts than on ourselves and our less obvious but more damaging acts of omission and indifference. More people and plant life die from our neglect and our overconsumption than from acts of terror.

So where does this leave us? Burdened with guilt but helpless? Sorry for what we are doing but not knowing what else to do? Yes, all of these things, but something else also comes to mind: repentance. The first step in behaving differently is admitting that we have not really and truly been asking God for a better world, not asking with our whole heart. Do we have the willingness to turn around, to change, to see ourselves and the world differently? This is an enormous question and would take a lifetime to answer, for we would have to live it, not just think it. But let us at least begin to think differently with the hope that we might also begin to live differently.

Throughout this book we have been asking the basic anthropological question: Who are we, and where do we fit in the scheme of things?

It is time now to summarize our findings on this issue as they relate to *action*. Who are we? Where do we fit on planet Earth? How do we get there?

Who Are We?

The Earth Charter, the United Nations document that emerged from a decade-long, worldwide, cross-cultural conversation about common goals and shared values, suggests a picture of who we are. It is a statement of fundamental principles for building a just, sustainable, and peaceful global society. It includes sixteen major principles, the first one being the most important: "Respect Earth and life in all its diversity." Spelled out in more detail, it advises, "Recognize that all beings are interdependent and every form of life has value regardless of its worth to human beings. Affirm faith in the inherent dignity of all human beings and in the intellectual, artistic, ethical, and spiritual potential of humanity." As I read these two sentences, they claim that all life, human and nonhuman, is valuable *as such*. There is here no separation of good and evil beings, nor the suggestion that some are worthwhile only because they are useful to others. The value of all life and the dignity of human beings comprise the first and most important principle in the Earth Charter. We have seen this same insistence on the intrinsic value of all life at the heart of the first creation story in the book of Genesis. What many remember from that story is that the text tells human beings to subdue and dominate the rest of creation, but while that command is given once, what is central to the story are the seven times God says, "It is good." After each act of creation—the sun, moon, stars, oceans, plants, animals, and finally human beings—God says, "It is good," ending with "It is very good." This is amazing—God appears to have an aesthetic appreciation for every scrap and tidbit of creation. God loves things for themselves, simply because they are. I think the philosopher Iris Murdoch was trying to express something similar when she wrote, "Love is the extremely difficult realization that something other than oneself is real. Love . . . is the discovery of reality."[1] What the Earth Charter, Genesis, and Iris Murdoch are suggesting is that the dignity of human beings and the integrity of creation rest on seeing everyone and everything as valuable, on seeing everything as "good" as God does. We want to see some people as good and some as bad, some parts of creation as useful to us and other parts as less useful. We want to think in dualisms, not continuities. But this new picture of who we are says that God loves—that is, recognizes the value of—each and every piece of creation.

If we were to begin to think this way about ourselves and other creatures, what might the consequences be? Recently, I have been reading and teaching about some of the people we call saints—people such as the Dalai Lama, Jean Vanier, Dorothy Day, Nelson Mandela, and Bishop Tutu. One outstanding characteristic of these people is their universal love—love that seems to know no bounds. It does not stop with their own family, tribe, race, country, or even species. All life is honored just because it exists. John Woolman, the eighteenth-century American Quaker and early abolitionist, describes his conversion experience in these terms. He writes that true religion consists in loving God the creator and willing justice and goodness to all people and even to "brute creatures," for he claims, "To say we love God as unseen, and at the same time exercise cruelty toward the least creature moving by [God's] life . . . is a contradiction in itself."[2] In other words, one cannot love God without loving all that God has made—to do otherwise is a contradiction. His conversion to what he calls "true religion" consists in a deepening love of God that results in the increase of "universal love to my fellow-creatures."

Another example is that of the Holocaust rescuers. Studies done on these people reveal that they did not hide and save Jews because they had any special preference for Jews; rather, they did so simply because they felt that every human being has the right to live.[3] Nor did they think that they did anything special: they thought that anyone in their position would have done the same thing. Of course, not everyone did. Not all people do see themselves and all other human beings, as well as creation itself, as valuable in and of themselves. Not everyone is truly a democrat when it comes to existence, as God is in Genesis.

The first movement we need to make in our commitment to think and act differently, then, is at the most fundamental level of who we think we are. The dignity of human beings and the integrity of creation rest, first of all, on our willingness to affirm the value of all life, not just our own or that of our own tribe or religion or country or class or species. Like the saints, we need to practice developing a universal love that knows no bounds, a love that becomes more and more inclusive. How far can it go? Jesus suggests that the stretch must include the enemy— that is certainly an interesting proposal.

We have seen that human dignity and the integrity of creation rest on a sensibility that respects the other, whether that other is a human being or a nonhuman aspect of creation. The most basic stance that we must take in order to live differently in the world is appreciation for something other than ourselves and our own interests. Like God, we need to be able to look at the world and say, "It is good." Period.

Where Do We Fit?

But a second movement is equally important and is in fact part of the first: all individuals, whether human beings, tigers, mountains, dandelions, apples, slugs, atoms, or elephants, exist only because of other things. In contrast to the Western belief that human beings are individuals who live *on* the earth, we in fact live *in* it. Moreover, we do not decide *when* we want to form relationships with other people and the earth, for we are *in* the most intimate and complex relationships from before our birth until after our death. Hence, the appreciation for each and every creature in creation—for its particularity and specialness and difference—does not mean a doctrine of "individualism" such as we see in our present Western culture. Just the opposite: individuals exist only in networks of interrelationship and interdependence.

This is one of the most important shifts needed in our view of ourselves if we are to make some progress in living appropriately in our time of climate change. Let us consider two insights about who we are and where we fit that come from the centrality of interrelationship. First, interrelationship says that everything is on a continuum. Since we and everything else in the universe evolved together from the Big Bang billions of years ago, we are all related—we are distant cousins to the stars, to oak leaves, and to deer. This means that we are like and unlike these others in mysterious and interesting ways. We want to think that humans are totally different from animals and plants—by thinking in terms of dualisms, we can use and misuse others. But nature operates in terms of continuities. Thinking on a continuum has profound implications for both human dignity and the integrity of creation: it means that all humans are intimately related to one another, whether they be male or female, black or white or brown, straight or gay, rich or poor, able-bodied or physically challenged, Muslim or Christian. The centrality of interrelationship means that regardless of whether other human beings are like us or not, and whether we like them or not, they *are* our relatives, our closest relatives, our nuclear family, if you will. It means that all other creatures are our relatives as well, even if distant cousins. The continuum also means that some people are not good and others evil, some are right and others wrong, some are healthy and others sick—we exist together in various shades and gradations. The edges are fuzzy that separate us from one another, and it is at these fuzzy edges that we often stretch out and touch each other.

It is with acceptance of the continuum of life that empathy develops. The saint's growing sense of universal love, love for *all* without exception, is not a momentary or mysterious insight. Rather, it develops in tandem with loving God; it is an extension of seeing God everywhere. As Woolman notes, one can't love God without loving all that God has made. The continuum of life is a reflection of the oneness of creation: we are called by God's love to universal love for all, a possibility that is based on the interdependence of all life. Hence, profound empathy with all forms of life is not a romantic fantasy; rather, it is based on the empirical evidence that *we are all interconnected and interdependent*.

The second insight about ourselves that emerges from the centrality of relationship concerns how the individual fits into the whole. It is easy for this to go wrong: for an individual to dominate the whole (as in totalitarianism) or for the whole to suffocate the individual (as in some fundamentalist cults). How can genuine individuality and radical relationship exist together? In the United States, the image of the melting pot unites all individuals into a somewhat bland similarity, whereas in Canada the mosaic allows individuals to be nicely differentiated but not very united. Ecological unity—the unity in which individuals exist *in* relationships and only in relationships—says that the whole is made up of the differences among individuals. In other words, individuality and unity depend on each other: an old-growth forest consists of millions of different plants and trees, insects and animals, each doing its job in order for the whole to be sustained. The whole is nothing but the healthy functioning of all the parts; hence, each and every part is valuable and necessary. Needless to say, this understanding of the whole and the parts has important implications for global economics as well as environmental standards. Justice and sustainability belong together: all of the parts must have the necessities of existence in order for the whole to survive. Justice to individuals—feeding people and sustaining plants—is not a choice that well-off people might make in a spirit of charity. Again, we see a correlation between ecology and saintly insight.

The saint's universal love for all is a necessity: it is based on the simple but radical insight that *others beside myself exist*. What appears to be a radical stance—inclusive love for all beings—is at one level simply good planetary economics. Justice at the level of the basics needed for the health of individuals, human and nonhuman, is a necessity: the whole cannot be sustained apart from the health of the parts. This sobering fact calls for a radical change in the behavior of those of us presently taking more than our share and, hence, causing other people and life-forms to deteriorate for lack of nourishment.

If we accept this picture of interrelationship and interdependence—the picture that puts us on a continuum with all other creatures and that claims that the whole can be healthy only if the parts are fed—then we have a very different understanding of ourselves than that depicted in our consumer culture and its consequence, climate change. That culture basically says that each of us human individuals has the right to all we can legally acquire—in fact, we owe it to ourselves to have the very best.

Once again, the saints have a very different view. In his Christmas sermon in 1967, Martin Luther King wrote, "As nations and individuals, we are interdependent . . . all caught up in an inescapable network of mutuality, tied into a single garment of human destiny."[4] We do not want to admit this truth, because acknowledging it demands too much of us. And yet King's view is what contemporary science is also telling us about our world. It is not just Christian piety that claims relationships are central, as in the Great Commandment to love God and neighbor. As Iris Murdoch puts it, "Love . . . is the discovery of reality." What a wonderful assertion that is! It tells us that loving others is not a sentimental religious teaching; rather, it is an objective statement about our world and where we fit into it. The individualistic view of capitalist consumerism is outmoded: it came from the eighteenth century, which discovered the importance of the individual (and for that we are grateful) but did not realize that individuals exist only in relationship.

We are beginning to see, perhaps, how the postmodern ecological view of who we are overlaps in crucial ways with the most profound insights from religion. Christianity is one of many religions that teaches love, empathy, compassion, and indeed sacrifice for the well-being of others. Both religion and ecology recognize the basic interconnection and interdependence of all life. Therefore, love toward others is the way things should be because it is based on the way things are. We need each other. What climate change is telling us loud and clear is that the days of radical individualism and its consumer culture are over; it is time to return to the roots of religion and the roots of life: *we are, all of us, in this together*.

How Do We Get There?

We are called to live in a different world, a world where the good of the individual and the good of the community are intrinsically and intimately related. But how do we get there? How do we even begin to live differently when our world is increasingly ordered around the greed of the individual and the decay of nature? Given what has happened since 9/11 in terms of hatred, violence, deception, war, imperialism, climate change, poverty, and AIDS, why even imagine such pictures, such visions of a different world? We return to Isa 65:24: "Before they call I will answer, while they are yet speaking I will hear." That is the only reason we dare to imagine a different world—because God is before us; God is there already. The world imagined by our biblical texts is not a fantasy; it is what the Jewish and Christian traditions tell us is God's will for us and promise to us. The one in whom we live and move and have our being assures us that this other world of appreciation for each and every individual creature living in networks of interrelationship and interdependence—that this world is not a dream but is the way things should be, and will be, with God's help. To the degree we live in God, from God, and for God, this world will emerge.

Now, fantastic as it sounds, this *is* what Jews and Christians, and in fact many religious people of other faiths, believe. God is in charge, and God wills a different world for all of us. As we turn now to the small steps we might take—what Isaiah says is our call to God—we listen to the wise words of Canadian activist Nellie McClung: "Let us do our little bit with cheerfulness and not take the responsibility that belongs to God. None of us can turn the earth around. All we can ever hope to do is to hit it a few whacks on the right side."[5] We will now consider a few whacks on the right side that might help us get to a different world.

Asking and Imagining

The first whack on the right side is to imagine and ask for a different world. But how can we break out of our conventional world to even imagine a different one? Jesus' parables are helpful at this point: they tell of people who were living conventional lives, only to have things turned upside down, inviting them into a new way of living. One thinks of the parables of the good Samaritan, the prodigal son, the rich ruler, the great dinner: in each of these stories, people's expectations about who is righteous, valuable, and important are abruptly derailed. The world that they knew is brought under sharp critique, and a different way of being in the world is presented: one in which foreigners, younger sons, poor people, and the marginalized are invited into God's favor. I think one of the most important things the parables suggest to us is that "a different world is possible." Mostly, we don't believe this—and why should we, given the horror we see all around us? Despair is the appropriate response for thoughtful, sensitive, good-hearted people.

If anything calls for despair, it is certainly global warming. In addition to the "ordinary" reasons for despair—war, violence, AIDS, greed, poverty, and plain old human indifference—now we are faced with the cataclysmic possibility of severe climate change, which will make any chance for a "different world" seemingly impossible. But Jesus was not a despairing type, though surely his world was equally awful. Rather, he had a great deal of what some anthropologists have called "wild space." Wild space is that part of each of us that doesn't quite fit into our conventional worlds; it is that part of our own personal world that doesn't completely overlap with the ordinary world—for us, this is the consumer market–oriented, individualistic, greedy world. Maybe we have some wild space because we are different in some way: poor, disabled, a person of color, a refugee, gay or lesbian, and so forth. Maybe we have some wild space because we have lived in an impoverished country and seen people without clean water or medicine, or maybe we have had a very rough childhood or recovered from a serious addiction. Whatever makes it possible to think outside the box, to think that things ought to be different—not just for oneself but for the world—is useful wild space. Jesus had a lot of wild space; in fact, we could say he was a *wild man*. He imagined what he called the kingdom of God, where this new pattern for living would come about—the pattern that Isaiah sums up in the wonderful words, "They shall not hurt or destroy on all my holy mountain." We *want* this different world. Peter Short, a past moderator of the United Church of Canada, puts it this way: "The residual memory of paradise is still in you, lingering like a scent of jasmine on a breeze. You are a paradise-haunted creature. If it were not so, why would you expect so much of the world? Why would you expect so much of yourself? See how you rage when hatred and greed and the desecration of the good earth make clear again and again that this is no paradise?"[6] Our wild space is the memory of where we came from and the hope of where we are going: from paradise to the kingdom of God, from living with all other creatures within the love of God to living once again all together within God's love. Nothing short of this will satisfy us. We come from paradise and yearn for the reign of God. Even global warming cannot change this longing and this hope.

To "see differently," to entertain the possibility of a different world, we must let our wild space come out from its hiding place. And then, in the magnificent words of Paul, we can begin to open ourselves to the glory of God, whose power working in us can do more than we can ask or imagine. *But we must ask and we must imagine.* This is, I think, the first and most important step toward living differently.

The question then arises, if we see ourselves differently, not as isolated individuals but as part of a vast network of valuable creatures who need and enjoy each other, will we begin to act that way? The Greeks said that to know the good is to do the good. If that were so, then our only challenge would be knowing who we are and where we fit—correct action would follow. But Paul wasn't so optimistic: he called himself a wretched man because he knew the good, but he didn't necessarily do it. There is no direct connection between knowing the good and doing the good. This is what the Christian tradition has called "sin"—being conscious of a better way but not choosing it. Moving beyond this paralysis is terribly difficult, especially when our culture rewards us for staying with a very different picture of who we are and what we ought to do. We do not have to commit active sins in order to contribute to the individualistic, greedy picture of human and planetary life that has resulted in climate change. All that we well-off North Americans have to do is to live like everyone else around us is living. The Christian tradition calls this the sin of omission rather than the sin of commission, and in many ways it is more insidious because we don't feel we have done anything bad. So how to move out of this place of denial and indifference?

One possibility is summed up in the Nike motto Just Do It. This perspective is in some ways the reverse of belief and action: it says to start with the action and the belief will follow. Many religious traditions stress action over belief: what you *do* matters more than what you *think*. Sometimes the most effective way of breaking out of paralysis, out of denial and indifference, is just to get on with it. The Jewish tradition is focused on people following the Torah, the law of God: living the truth is of primary importance. The saints of the church seem to agree: Teresa of Avila, a sixteenth-century nun, suggested that if you are not certain about your relationship with God, stop worrying about it, focus on loving your neighbor, and the God-question will take care of itself. Latin American liberation theologians claim that theology needs a fundamental revolution, a shift from its traditional focus on orthodoxy to a new focus on orthopraxy—from concern with right belief to right action. As they often say, "To know Jesus is to love Jesus." Or in the words of Gustav Gutierrez, "We find the Lord in our encounters with [human beings], especially the poor, marginalized, and exploited ones. An act of love toward them is an act of love toward God."[7]

In regard to global warming and the lifestyle changes that are necessary, living the truth is the way to begin. We do not need more information; what we need is to cut through our indifference and denial. Sometimes the smallest steps are an opening: in interesting ways, the humble task of faithful recycling can be the beginning toward a raise in consciousness as well as wider and deeper actions. A person and a society can live their way into the truth, even when they do not at the outset fully comprehend or accept that truth. Live differently and a different world may become possible.

In summary, following Nellie McClung's advice, our first good whack on the right side of the world is to imagine and ask for a different world, to dare go with our wild space about what is possible, and then to start to live differently, in whatever halting and limited ways we can.

Material Well-Being

A second whack on the right side of the world is for us to focus not on the spiritual but on the material well-being of others. Why should we do this? For two reasons: First, an incarnational religion demands that we pay attention to the flesh, the body, the most basic needs of others. Second, by focusing on the material needs of others, we begin to see how much our own level of material well-being keeps us from seeing differently. To expand on the first reason: Christianity claims that the divine became human and dwells among us—flesh of our flesh, in and of the earth. It seems like an outrageous claim: How could (or should) the transcendent God become one with us, with all flesh, with the earth itself? However, it is not an outrageous claim if one believes that God is not distant, supernatural, but rather the one in whom we live and move and have our being, the one from whom all life comes and to whom all life returns. It was not outrageous to Isaiah, whose God answers before we even call, who hears us before we have finished speaking. This God does not seem to care so much about our spiritual or religious needs as about our ordinary ones: long life, houses to live in, food to eat, enjoyable work, healthy children, peace and well-being among all creatures. How mundane! Indeed. An incarnate God is exactly that: mundane. I think this God cares about entire species of animals becoming extinct because humans grab all the land; God cares about children who do not have fresh water to drink; God cares about polar bears who are dying because of shrinking ice floes; God cares about the fact that North Americans who make up 5 percent of the world's population use 25 percent of its energy resources.

An incarnate religion demands an incarnate spirituality; one could call it "spirituality of the body." Hence, issues of global warming become religious issues: clean air and water, food and shelter, become "works of the spirit." When life is seen as intrinsically valuable and all life exists in networks of interrelationship and interdependence, then there is no split between spirit and flesh, with religion concerned mainly with the spirit. An incarnate religion refuses to allow well-off people to pacify the poor with promises of eternal life, while their ordinary lives lack the necessities for a decent existence. This is seen for what it is: an ingenious maneuver by those of us with ample material goods to deny them to other needy human beings and life-forms.

Turning to the saints again for insight, we find that they appear to do exactly what most of us do not: they see the material condition of others as a spiritual matter. If we think of Francis of Assisi, Dorothy Day, John Woolman, Jean Vanier, Simone Weil, or Nelson Mandela, we discover that the body and its needs are their central concern. These saints do not work to save the souls of the poor for the sweet by-and-by, but put their own bodies on the line so that the ordinary, mundane needs of other human beings might be met. For these people, the material condition of others is a spiritual matter. Their universal love that knows no bounds is an earthly, bodily love. Issues such as climate change, which directly affect the health of bodies—human ones as well as other life-forms—become from this perspective heinous sins, much worse sins than our minor personal moral failures. What matters is how we live day by day and whether the way we live helps the material condition of others. The winner of the Nobel Peace Prize for 2004, Wangari Maathai, has lived such a life. For three decades she has been instrumental in planting more than thirty million trees in deforested parts of Africa. As the Nobel committee realized, "peace" is not just the cessation of wars; more basically, it is about providing the earth and its people with the basics of existence.

But *how* can we learn to see the material needs of others as a spiritual matter? John Woolman sold his profitable grocery business because he was making too much money. The money kept him from seeing clearly; he said that he wanted his eye to be single so he could see things as they really are, but he kept seeing double because his own material wealth was squarely in his line of sight. When he got himself and his money out of the center, he could see the relationship between slavery and wealth: in order for some people to live lavishly, they were willing to enslave others. Without the lavish lifestyle, might they have been able to see differently—perhaps with their "wild space"? Global warming is an unusually strong call to develop our wild space. The dire consequences predicted from climate change invite us to open ourselves to radically new ways of thinking and living on our planet. The wisdom of most religious traditions advising self-denial may be radical, but it is not negative. Rather, self-denial allows our wild side— the ability to see differently and hence to live differently—to emerge. Self-denial is not principally about ascetic flagellation; rather, it is often the first step toward developing a universal love of others, toward seeing all others as valuable and as interrelated.

But looking at the lives of the saints, while highly instructive, can also lead to despair. Francis of Assisi gave away *all* of his possessions, not only to clothe and feed others, but also to attain spiritual poverty: the poverty of radical humility, of radical openness to God and all other creatures. We are not likely to do this. In fact, stories like those of Woolman and Francis can turn us away: *we* can't be saints, so we might as well do nothing. German theologian Dorothee Soelle, writing about mysticism and resistance, says, "The retreat of a Thomas Merton to the solitude of a Trappist monastery is not that far removed from an annual intervention in a shareholder's meeting."[8] She notes that in the United States today, more than $450 billion is invested in line with ethical criteria rather than maximum profit. The people insisting on the ethical investments are not Francis of Assisi nor engaged in a revolution, but they are *resisting*. Resisters engage in acts of self-denial, of limitation, of saying no, of standing firm, of resisting the temptation of more, of refusing to join the crowd. Resisters can be as modest as a child who recycles or as bold as those who speak out at a stockbrokers' meeting. What matters is the clarity of vision that comes from stepping out from the blinders that our consumer culture puts on us so that we begin to see differently.

Perseverance

And this leads us to a third good whack on the right side: perseverance. Our small acts of resistance, of saying no to more, of refusing to go with the crowd, will not save the world, but they can help us see the material needs of others as our spiritual task. They can help us see global warming as a religious issue. I have suggested that a vision of all life as valuable and interdependent can come about for us if we open ourselves to seeing differently—to letting our wild side imagine such a world and to limiting our own material worth so that we may see better and so that others may have more. Now I suggest that the important thing is to "hang in there." Ecological despair is one of the most difficult problems for us as we try to change—to see differently and to live differently. By "ecological despair," I mean the crushing sense of futility that comes over us the more we learn about the state of our world and its creatures. Global warming is raising ecological despair several notches. Every time we open a newspaper, we read more grim statistics: the Arctic is melting, China opens new coal plants every week, extreme weather events are becoming common, the temperature in Labrador in the spring of 2007 reached 34°C.

It all seems so overwhelming. Why bother? When I want to turn away in despair and give up, I am brought up short by a remark by Dorothy Day, who spent forty years in one of the poorest areas of New York City. Of people who called her a saint, she said, "Don't dismiss me so easily"—meaning, *Don't let yourself off the hook so fast.* She claimed that to live as she did does not require great talent or courage, but mostly hard work. "I have done nothing well," she said. "But I have done what I could."[9] Indeed. Those who study the lives of the saints emphasize the ordinariness of becoming a saint: as one says, "Goodness is banal as training for something is banal."[10] In other words, living differently from the world is a habit one develops; people are not born good—or saintly—they become so through small, daily, continual changes in behavior and insight. Seeing differently and behaving differently appear for those most successful at it to be a cyclical process of small but persevering decisions. Most of us do not want to consider the banality of goodness, just as we don't want to accept the banality of evil—that people like Hitler and Saddam Hussein are ordinary people, not demons. We would prefer to see the very good people or the very bad ones as saints or demons; then when we read their stories, the finger does not point to us. We cannot be that good or that bad, we say, but we can be better or worse. I like the following bits of advice: Confucius said, "It does not matter how slow you go, as long as you don't stop"; T. S. Eliot adds: "Only those who risk going too far can possibly find out how far one can go."[11]

We have been reflecting on whether, given global warming, a different world is possible. Can human dignity and the integrity of creation survive what we are facing? We have asked this question by focusing on three questions: Who are we? Where do we fit on planet Earth? and How do we get there? As we come to the end of our thoughts for now, I would like to put these reflections in perspective by suggesting two qualifications. The first qualification is that in focusing on questions of who we think we are in the scheme of things—the worldview we hold—we have looked only at one small, though I think important, issue. Our subject of living with human dignity and upholding the integrity of creation in a time of global warming is huge—it includes the entire planetary agenda, that is, what all people must do in every field of endeavor, every religion, every aspect of their daily lives so that things can get better. As people of faith, we are charged with the crucial task of helping people change at the level of their most basic assumptions about who we are and thus how we should act in the world. This is one of the primary functions of religion: forming these profound and often unconscious beliefs. That is what we have focused on here, but it is just one thing that needs to be done.

The second qualification on our reflections is to return us to our Isaiah passage. The presumption of trying to think differently, let alone act differently, is possible only because our religious traditions tell us the marvelous news that God answers before we call, that God hears before we speak. We are not alone. The dream we have for a new world, a new earth, is not just our dream; it is the dream of God, and God has placed this dream within each one of us. The dream of paradise and the dream of the kingdom of God are finally why we keep going and how we keep going. We are paradise-haunted creatures who yearn for the kingdom of God. We hang in there because God hangs in there. Hallelujah!

9

"The DEAREST FRESHNESS DEEP DOWN THINGS": The HOLY SPIRIT and CLIMATE CHANGE

God's Grandeur
The world is charged with the grandeur of God.
*   It will flame out, like shining from shook foil;*
*   It gathers to a greatness, like the ooze of oil*
Crushed. Why do men then now not reck his rod?
Generations have trod, have trod, have trod;
*   And all is seared with trade; bleared, smeared with toil*
*   And wears man's smudge and shares man's smell: the soil*
Is bare now, nor can foot feel, being shod.

And for all this, nature is never spent;
*   There lives the dearest freshness deep down things;*
And though the last lights off the black West went
*   Oh, morning, at the brown brink eastward, springs—*
Because the Holy Ghost over the bent
*   World broods with warm breast and with ah! bright wings.*
—Gerard Manley Hopkins[1]

Twenty-five years ago, a conversation about the Holy Ghost rescued me from an embarrassing social event. I was sitting across from the wife of Italy's ambassador to England at a high table dinner at an Oxford college. I was definitely out of my comfort zone and wondered how I could manage over the next several hours of elaborate cuisine, copious wine, and clever conversation. The ambassador's wife asked me what I "did." I hesitated, knowing that "being a theologian" is comparable to "being a nuclear physicist" to most people. But I mumbled what I "did." She smiled warmly and replied, "You know, when I was a child, I always prayed to the Holy Ghost because I figured he was less busy than the other two." The rest of the evening was a smashing success.

But within this story lies an interesting historical note: the Holy Ghost (Spirit) has been the neglected third party of the Trinity—at least until about fifty years ago. Even in my own early writing, I disparaged the "spirit" metaphor as "amorphous, vague, and colorless," "ethereal, shapeless, and vacant," concluding that "Spirit is not a strong candidate for imaging God's sustaining activity."[2] But how wrong I was! I should have known better, since I have loved Hopkins's poem about the Holy Ghost since I was in college. However, it was only recently as I reread the poem in the light of climate change that it began to take on new depth and meaning for me.

"God's Grandeur," written in 1877, bemoans nature's fate at the hands of Western industrialism: the separation of human beings from nature via shoes and the desecration of nature by human activity ("seared with trade"). What should be a world "charged" with God's glory, so that every single scrap of creation tells of God in its own way, has become smudged, bleared, and smeared, camouflaging the particular reflection of God in all things. Hopkins's vision of God and the world in which each and every iota of creation shines with some aspect of divine glory has faded in the last lights of a dark Western culture. But the hope for the "bent world" does not lie in nature's own restorative powers; rather, it rests in the warm breast and bright wings of the Holy Ghost. God's power of motherly brooding that hovered over the chaotic waters at creation is with us still in the bright, rising wings of each new morning. In this poem we have an argument for, a confession of, hope. Hopkins could not envision the destruction of nature that we now know, and which is epitomized in global warming, but the witness of this poem is that *no matter how bad things get*, there is hope—not because of human beings or even of nature, but because the power of life and love that was at the beginning of creation is with us still as our source and our savior. "Nature is never spent" and "there lives the dearest freshness deep down things" *because* of the sustaining power and love of God's Spirit. The sextet of the sonnet could not be stronger, more intimate, or more hopeful. We who can now imagine, given climate change, the end of civilization as we know it, brought about by Western carbon dioxide emissions, shiver at the ominous line, "the last lights off the black West went," but take a breath of hope with the final three lines. Here, the "bent world," our world indeed, is nonetheless the place where divine love is incubating new life after the terrible destruction we have brought to our planet. Like a mother bird tucking the new life under her own body and earnestly protecting it, God sustains and renews us, *no matter what.* The final four words are more than we could ask or imagine: "with ah! bright wings." We do not deserve this; we could not have expected it; we can scarcely believe it, but it is the one thing necessary as we face up to climate change and the needed changes in our behavior.

Surely, this image of God is the one for our time. Nothing less can speak to the depth of our despair as we well-off humans contemplate what we are doing through our reckless, selfish, out-of-control consumerism to the poor of the planet and to the planet itself. We now know that climate change, which will affect every plant, animal, and person on earth, is the most serious crisis of the twenty-first century. If we ever thought ourselves in charge of the earth, capable of "managing" the planet, we now know that we have failed utterly. We must undergo the deepest of all conversions, the conversion from egocentricism to theocentrism, a conversion to what we truly are: reflections of God, as is everything in creation. The only difference between us and the rest of creation is that the others reflect God, tell of God, simply by being, whereas we must *will* that it be so. We must desire to be what we truly are—made in the image of God, and thus able to live justly and sustainably on earth with all other creatures.

God and the World:
A Sacramental Sensibility

The reason for Hopkins's hopefulness is his belief that the world lives within God. Hopkins has a sacramental religious sensibility: God and the world are not two separate realities that exist independently and must somehow find each other. Rather, the world is "charged" with God as if with electricity. "All things therefore are charged with love, are charged with God and if we know how to touch them give off sparks and take fire, yield drops and flow, ring and tell of him."[3] Hopkins's sacramental sensibility, in which each scrap of creation becomes *more itself* as it lives more completely within God, can most adequately be expressed with the metaphor of "spirit." God is the empowering Spirit who brings all things to fulfillment, or in a gloss on Irenaeus, "The glory of God is all things fully alive." This is not a view of the God-world relationship in which the more power the one has, the less the other has; rather, God is the "wild air, world-mothering air" in which all things grow and flourish.[4] Hopkins agrees with the medieval mystic Mechthild of Magdeburg: "The day of my spiritual awakening was the day I saw—and knew I saw—all things in God and God in all things." We live within God; hence, metaphors such as water, breath, milieu, ocean, and air are our weak attempts to express the utter dependence *and* radical uniqueness that lie at the heart of an incarnational understanding of creation. This understanding says that we live within the body of God; that the world is/is not the body of God; that all things exist within the one reality that is, and that reality is on the side of life and its fulfillment. God as Spirit is the power of life and love within which all bodies exist. Most creatures live instinctively as the sacraments they were meant to be: they reflect God's glory, each in its own illimitable way. We humans have a choice: to live in reality, in and for God, or to live in and for ourselves—nowhere—outside of reality. We have the choice *to live a lie*, to live what we were not meant to be, in and for ourselves.

This ontology—the world within God—provides a picture of the God-world relationship that is the ground of our hope. It gives a reason to hope at a time when our planet seems doomed to destruction. Let us look at some of the features of this picture of God and the world.

Who Is God?

If the world exists within God—if in the lovely words of Julian of Norwich, God holds the world as one holds a hazelnut in one's hand—then God is everywhere. God is either everywhere or nowhere. God cannot be in "one place" and not "another place"; a "being" might do that, but not God. God is right under the surface in everything. God "accompanies" us when we travel to the ends of the earth—we may have to leave our loved ones behind, but not God. Moreover, prayer is merely the acknowledgment that God is always there, always available. *We* may not be present; in fact, we are often absent, but God is always present. God the Spirit is ubiquitous, everywhere at the same time, always hovering with warm breast over every inch of the earth (universe). God is the liminal presence in all things. The divine presence announces itself in a breeze rustling through leaves, in the sound of a bird's call, in the face of a starving child (or a happy one), in a clear-cut forest. God is in all things because all things are in God—in all shapes and shades, all conditions and crises, all joys and sorrows. God is in birth and death and everything in between. God is ubiquitous: God is wherever I am, wherever each and every iota of creation is.

But God is not a being, even the highest being: God is reality. This is another way of saying God is "being itself," or the ground of all that is real, is actual, exists. The Christian tradition can lead us astray when it suggests that God is a supernatural being who is the only reality. This paradigm suggests unilateral divine power, power that takes over and sucks everything into itself. Here God is both not great enough and too great: not the source of all life and love, but the highest being, the only power in the universe, choking off all other powers. But if God is reality, in whom we find our own distinctive realities, then trees can still be trees and mountains can be mountains and even I can and must be myself. God is the Spirit, the breath, the ether, the atmosphere in which each and every thing grows and flourishes. Here there is no competition for power: the world is charged with the grandeur of God, and it is so by *being most fully itself*. God as the body of the world *is* that body by way of all the zillions of bodies that compose the universe. There is one reality: God visible (body) and invisible (spirit), but the latter is known *through* the former. Everything is suffused, infused, with God's breath and light and power. The world is alive with God—but indirectly, incarnationally.

Christian mysticism—seeing God in all things and all things in God—is incarnational. We live *in God through the world*. Everything exists within God's "womb," within God as womb. This womb, the earth, is the body from which we derive breath, food, water, and habitat. There is not God *and* the world, but the world *as it exists and only exists in God*. We become aware of God *through the earth*: we develop "double vision," the ability to see God *in* the world, in its beauty and its horror, and even in the most ordinary things on ordinary days. Mysticism is this double vision, seeing everything as it is *and* as in God, both at the same time. Mysticism is radical incarnationalism, seeing God in the flesh *everywhere*. Mysticism is delight in things and in God; it is seeing, hearing, tasting, smelling, touching God everywhere and in everything, but *only* in and through all of these wonderful creatures. Who would want a disembodied mysticism? "The world is charged with the grandeur of God"—indeed, it is. God is in all things incarnationally: God tells us of life, love, truth, beauty, and goodness as each of these qualities is realized in the world. Thus, the exquisite beauty of an alpine forget-me-not is the way we experience God's beauty; the energy and joy of a young child is the way we experience God's vitality and life. "Everything is God," God is reality, but *only* as everything is exquisitely, precisely, idiosyncratically itself. "The glory of God is every creature fully alive." God and the world are not in competition: an incarnational theology does not say, "The more God, the less world," or "The more world, the less God." Rather, it says, "The more God, the more world," and vice versa. We, the world, flourish *in* God, *only* in God, and *fully* in God.

God is not a being, then, but reality: God is the "stuff" out of which everything comes and to which it will return. Life emanates from God and is more "like God" than like anything else. All creation was made in God's image, as a reflection of God, and this is what we humans must acknowledge and live into. There is not "God and the world," but "God and God in the form of the world" (the world as God's body, God's incarnation). The world (all matter) is a manifestation of God, for God is reality. If the world were "outside" God, then there would be something greater than God, that is, "God and the world." A dictionary definition of *reality* is "something that exists independently of all other things and from which other things derive."[5] Hence, "God" is being-itself, or existence-itself, the source of all other forms of existence. So, to say that God is reality is not to say that God contains or includes all that is in a pantheistic fashion. Rather, it is to say that God is that from which all else derives its being, its reality. If we then say that reality is "good," we make a faith statement about the hopeful, life-giving direction of what "really is," in contrast to appearances, which do not support such a statement.

And this is the most astounding thing of all—that reality is good, that God is love. God is in, with, and for everything. The "with" and "for" part is what Christians read about reality in the face of Jesus: in his ministry of love and healing and in his death for the oppressed, Christians claim that reality (God) is on the side of life and its fulfillment. This is the "direction" of reality, something we could not figure out on our own; in fact, most evidence appears to be contrary. God is like Jesus: "For it is the God who said, 'Let light shine out of darkness,' who has shone in our hearts to give the light of the knowledge of the glory of God in the face of Jesus Christ" (2 Cor 4:6). Thus, reality (God) is not a being, but is "personal" in that we can use words such as *love* and *fulfillment* regarding reality's "intention." This assertion about reality's intention is what faith, rock-bottom faith, is: trust that love and not indifference, neutrality, or malevolence is at the heart of things. It is not "belief in God," but trust that things will be all right or, in Julian's words, "all things shall be well."

Another way to express this understanding of the God-world relationship is the Trinity—not the conundrum of "three persons in one substance," but the truth that God (reality) is a giving and a receiving God. The Trinity suggests what reality is: a continual flow of giving and receiving, of sharing, of living in one another, of counting on one another. We see a form of this reality in ecology: the interrelationship and interdependence of all things. Nothing is itself alone—even God, or perhaps most eminently, God. In the beginning was relationship, so says the Trinity. There is no beginning or end to this process—no self (God or creature) that is itself by itself. We become through relationship—with God and with our billions of neighbors. The Trinity reminds us that God is not an isolated individual—nothing is. Thus, God is not a being outside of other things; rather, God is the reality of all things, or all things become real (exist and are fulfilled) by living in God. Trying to live anywhere else is false, a lie, hopeless. Things *are* themselves as and to the extent they acknowledge the source of their being. This is an extraordinary thought: life and grace are the same thing. Grace is the gift of acknowledging one's total dependence on God, who is life and gives life.

Who Are We?

If God is reality, in whom we live and move and have our being, from whom we come and to whom we return, then our time on earth is also lived within God. We are not on our own; we belong to God. Believing in God is not primarily asserting that "God exists"; rather, it is acknowledging that I know who I am. I am a contingent, unnecessary, transient creature who has been given the gift of life and love. I am aware of being totally and gratefully dependent on the earth and all its interlocking support systems, on others whom I love and who love me, and on whatever is in, through, with, and for life and love—what we call "God." I did not create myself; I cannot sustain myself; I cannot transform myself. I live within the womb that gives me birth, feeds and nurtures me, gives me delight and joy, strengthens me through loss and suffering, and will be my tomb when I die.

Remembering daily and in particular ways who I am and where I fit in the scheme of things is a central spiritual discipline. Coming to faith is not so much knowing who God is as knowing who I am. I am not the center of things; I do not live by my own merit or means; I am finite, mortal, and small. And yet coming to faith as this dependent, vulnerable creature means that I trust ("know") that I live in God: God is my reality. I am not on my own; I cannot account for my own existence, let alone its moments of flourishing, from myself. I belong to something outside of myself that is at the same time inside and all around me. I belong to the source of my breath, my delight, my need, my hope. And in pain, loss, sorrow, disappointment—and even destruction and death—I still belong to God, though I often do not know how.

The acknowledgment of who we are (our "faith") means a dual realization: of gratitude and responsibility, of delight and duty. The primary religious emotions are wonder, amazement, and thankfulness. Simply to be alive, along with all of the other fascinating, diverse, beautiful, and wonderful creatures is a gift beyond imagining. Once we wake up to the glory of planet Earth in all its spectacular particularity and complexity, we are blown away. Once we "see" the world—and ourselves as part of it—with "double vision," as grounded in God and resplendent with the individuality of each thing, from slugs to forget-me-nots, from whales to big cedars, from crouching tigers to fields of waving wheat, we want to shout, "Hallelujah!" To see creatures, including human beings, becoming their illimitable selves *as* they live within and for God—this is a great joy. We realize that there is no either/or, but a both/and: it is not God versus us, but rather God as the ground, source, breath, water, womb, bath, air, breast, and tomb within which we become who we truly are. Each scrap of creation, including us human beings, becomes the unique individual that in its own distinctive way tells of God's glory.

And our peculiar, distinguishing characteristic is seen in the choice that we humans have to tell of God. We are the one creature that has to decide to reflect God. What is becoming increasingly clear is that the way we must reflect God is to accept responsibility for planetary well-being. Accepting this responsibility is an awesome task. Never before have human beings *known* that they are responsible for planetary health. Until the second half of the twentieth century, human beings could, with good conscience, still claim that our behavior might not be the cause of the earth's increasing deterioration. But that is no longer the case. The first step in accepting responsibility as God's partner in sustaining creation's health is to admit that *we* are a major cause of the crisis facing the twenty-first century: global warming. Denial is no longer possible. This first step is finally occurring, even in Western governments and oil companies.

The second step is to become informed about climate change. Doing so is not easy. Global warming is an incredibly complex phenomenon; in fact, it involves the most complicated, profound, and important systems on earth. It has no one cause; it has many feedback systems; and it has some unknowns. It is not something we *want* to be responsible for—any more than the generation that fought the Second World War wanted to do so. But it is our calling, our destiny, and our duty. It is the planetary agenda that faces all people, all religions, all fields of expertise, all professions of our time. The consequences of global warming will reach into every corner of the earth, from the decline of biodiversity to the desertification of land, from the spread of tropical disease to the flooding of cities, from the melting of ice caps to wars over food and water and the retreat of the wealthy to fortified spaces as the poor cry at the gates. The prospect of the earth's future in light of uncontrolled global warming by a number of sources is frightening, if not terrifying. But do we have a choice? Once we see who we are in the scheme of things—the neediest of all creatures and dependent on our planet's health for every breath we take, every cup of water we drink, every piece of food we eat—we realize that we *must* take care of the earth that is taking care of us.

One of the central tasks for the world's religions, including Christianity, is to attend to the image of human beings that functions in our society. Anthropology, the study of human beings and their place in the scheme of things, is the business of religion. Religions are central in forming the most basic assumptions about God and the world, and especially about human beings, for the cultures in which they exist. It is for this reason that we have undertaken in these pages a Christian vision of God and the world that is both deep within the tradition and relevant to our time. *If* people were to see themselves as living within God along with and for all other creatures, might we not have a vision of humanity that would encourage both responsibility and hope? Would we not see that *we are not alone*; rather, we are part of a magnificent creation in which all creatures are interdependent and all radically dependent on the source of their life and well-being? Would we not take courage—along with the great responsibility we now feel—*because* "there lives the dearest freshness deep down things," the Spirit of God, whose warm breast and bright wings are the hope of planet Earth?

What Is Our Task? Care and Hope

Surely, the most difficult task facing us as we finally acknowledge our responsibility for planetary health is summed up in one small word: *hope*. Is it possible to have any? The more we learn of climate change—the apocalyptic future that awaits us unless we make deep, speedy changes in our use of fossil fuels—the more despairing we become. Whether it is a 50 percent, 70 percent, or 90 percent reduction in carbon dioxide emissions worldwide that must be reached by 2050, it is a task that seems beyond our physical—and more important, our moral and emotional—capacity. It appears that we human beings do not have the *will* to live differently—justly and sustainably—to the degree necessary to save ourselves and our planet. The single most difficult obstacle to overcome is, then, our own lack of hope. This issue cannot be brushed aside. It is important to face the facts.

Increasingly, in popular media such as films and novels, we see pictures of the dystopia that awaits us in a future of profound environmental degradation. It will not be a world simply of less water, more heat, and fewer species of plants and animals; rather, it will be one of violent class wars over resources, the breakdown of civilization at all levels, and the end of certain facets of ordinary life that we have come to expect—the opportunity to have meaningful work, to raise healthy children, to enjoy leisure activities.

"Life as we know it," as we well-off North Americans have come to expect as "natural" and as our "right," will come to an end. The most ordinary activities that rely on access to basic resources will disappear:

going to school, putting on parties, enjoying concerts, taking vacations, watering the flowers. The ordinary things that make up the fabric of our days and that we love are at stake. An environmental dystopia will be not only piles of garbage in the streets, violent gangs of thugs, new dangerous diseases, and constant fear for one's safety. It also will be the fraying of the most basic civilities between people, the undermining of solidarity and community, and in its place we can expect a raw, radical, and very sad form of individualism.

As we imagine this dystopia, as we begin to feel what life will be like on a daily basis, we are horrified. Most people do not allow themselves to imagine this possibility, claiming that it is an exaggeration, that human ingenuity can cope with the situation. But dismissal of the facts is becoming increasingly difficult: denial and rationalization appear to have had their day. We must allow our imaginations to begin to live within the world that responsible science is telling us will be our fate unless drastic changes are made soon. We must do this so that we can acknowledge where our hope really resides—not with us, but in the power of love and renewal that lives within the universe, the Holy Spirit, the Spirit of God.

As we consider the basis for our hope, let us recall who God is. We must and can change our ways, live justly and sustainably on our planet, because of God, not because of ourselves. The hope we have lies in the radical transcendence of God, a transcendence so transcendent that it exceeds all of our notions of transcendence. A "supernatural" transcendence—God as the highest being who controls the world—is a paltry view of transcendence compared with God as radically immanent to and with and for *everything that is*. God's transcendence—God's power of creative, redeeming, and sustaining love—is closer to us than we are to ourselves. God is the milieu, the source, of power and love in which our world, our fragile, deteriorating world, exists. The world is not left to fend for itself, nor is God "in addition" to anything, everything. Rather, God *is* the life, love, truth, goodness, and beauty that empower the universe and shine out from it. God is the reality of everything that is; hence, without God, nothing would be. Therefore, God is always present, always here (and there); we simply have to open ourselves to become aware of and acknowledge God's presence. This is the basis of our hope: the world is created, loved, and "kept" by God, as Julian puts it.

Thus, "mysticism" is simply this awareness of God's presence in and through and with everything for its well-being. Mysticism is not—or need not be—a one-on-one relationship between a human individual and God; rather, it is the acknowledgment that everything lives and thrives and rejoices—and grieves and dies—*in* God. Mysticism is radical incarnationalism, seeing God in the flesh *everywhere* and in all conditions of embodied life. Mysticism is the recognition that we are never alone—nothing is—for God is ubiquitous.

Julian's lovely story of the hazelnut sums up our hope: hope for the world lies with God, its maker, lover, and keeper.

> At the same time, he [God] showed me something small, about the size of a hazelnut, that seemed to lie in the palm of my hand as round as a tiny ball. I tried to understand the sight of it, wondering what it could possibly mean. The answer came: "This is all that is made." I felt it was so small that it could easily fade to nothing; but again I was told, "This lasts and it will go on lasting forever because God loves it. And so it is with every being that God loves." I saw three properties about this tiny object. First, God had made it; second, God loves it; and third, God keeps it. And yet what this really means to me, that he is the Maker, the Keeper, the Lover, I cannot begin to tell.[6]

This is the religious sensibility that allows us to hope, a sensibility that imagines the world as a hazelnut, held within divine love, trusting not in its own powers to "last," but in the never-ending creative, redeeming, and sustaining love of God. Surely we feel about our sorry, beleaguered planet as Julian did holding the hazelnut: "I felt it was so small that it could easily fade to nothing," but she was told that it *will survive* because God loves it. This is certainly an astounding statement of faith, a statement of radical hope. Hope is trust, trust in God—not in things, events, or people. To trust in God means God can be counted on to hold one's life and all life in trust, in safekeeping. It means that one can rest one's life—and the life of the whole planet—in God, knowing that this trust will *somehow* be honored. Although, as Julian acknowledges, what it means to say God makes, loves, and keeps the world, we "cannot begin to tell."

This, then, is an odd kind of hope. It does not mean that things will necessarily turn out "as we hope," nor does it mean that we will be successful in our attempts to "save" the planet, but it does mean that God will "make all things well," as Julian writes in her mysterious, enigmatic, and profoundly hopeful words. "It was in this way that our Good Lord answered all questions and doubts I might make, comforting me greatly with these words: 'I may make all things well; I can make all things well, and I will make all things well, and I shall make all things well; and you shall see for yourself that all manner of things shall be well.'"[7] Faith in God is the conviction that since everything lives within God—that the reality we inhabit is love—things will be "all right." But this sounds absurd, if not morally repugnant. How can "things be well" if people and the planet are dying from global warming? We do not know. We believe, however, that it is so, not because we will make it so, but because of God. This is not a sentimental or romantic hope that things will turn out okay, but rather the faith that *however they turn out*, the world and all its creatures are held, kept, within God.

Since reality is oriented, however obscurely, mysteriously, and circuitously, to the world's well-being, we *can* hope. We live toward this future, because we already know something of it—if we did not, we could not hope. We know it every day as "morning, at the brown brink eastward, springs." The small glimmers we have of hope—the return of flowers, the birth of a child, a compassionate deed—make us certain that this is the way things were meant to be and will be, *because* these reflections of God's love are shining forth in our world. Having hope is a sign that we are already on our way: we cannot know God apart from God; we cannot hope in God apart from the gifts of hope that God gives us in the most ordinary—and precious—moments of our lives. If we have hope, we have all things, for trusting in God means that nothing can separate us from the source of power and love in the universe.

Curiously, this faith, not in ourselves, but in God, can free us to live lives of radical change. Perhaps it is the only thing that can. We do not rely on such hope as a way to escape personal responsibility—"Let God do it"—but rather this hope frees us from the pressure of outcomes so that we can add our best efforts to the task at hand. It allows for a measure of detachment from goals so that we can focus on doing our part. It allows us also to reflect on God's way of loving the world, a way expressed in the Christian doctrines of incarnation, cross, and resurrection: God loves the world totally and completely. God gives everything, goes the limit, to be on the side of life and its fulfillment. But God does this in a way suited to us embodied beings who live in our physical "house." The story of Jesus Christ is the story of God incarnate, facing the worst that the world (human beings) can offer in terms of oppression and destruction, and rising to new life—the cross and the resurrection. It is a story that goes *through* physical horror, physical death: it is inclusive of the worst dystopia that we, in the twenty-first century, can imagine for our deteriorating planet—and yet it is the story of "the dearest freshness deep down things," of the bright wings of the Holy Spirit. The two major days of the Christian calendar—Christmas and Easter—are about hope and renewal. They are about new life. Christmas is the celebration of birth, the incarnation of God in the world; Easter is the celebration of rebirth, the world's rebirth. The resurrection is a yes to life against death, or perhaps more accurately, it is the recognition that death and life, life and death, are parts of God, who is all yes. Even death takes place within the Great Yes (though what this means, we "cannot begin to tell").

So on the one hand, it appears that it is impossible to despair, since we live (and even die) within God, within reality, which is love. Whether we are joyful or despairing, healthy, sick, alive, or dead, we live in love. Nothing can be totally negative or final or fearful (even despair and death), because everything happens *within* God's love. There is always hope that something else, something more, something good might happen (yes, even in death), because we live and die in God's world. In a sense, then, everything that happens, good or bad, happens to God also. There are no scraps, no leftovers, no tail ends of creation that do not rest in God; nothing is neglected or passed over.

But on the other hand, what of the evil, perverse, murderous, greedy events that we humans are responsible for? Even here, God is present—not as the power behind such events, but as the negative critique of them. God is incarnate as the Yes beneath all that is life and love and goodness and truth and beauty, and as the No in all that is cruel, perverse, false, greedy, and hateful. To practice the presence of God means to embrace what God embraces: life and love. But we must not shy from imagining the worst possible outcome of human behavior, a sickening, hopeless dystopia, and then we must put even this picture of the world where it belongs—within God. Whatever happens to us and to our world, however horrendous, happens to God as well. We are cupped within the divine hands, warmed in the divine breast, held close through our greatest fears, comforted when things go wildly wrong. If this were not the case, then we are indeed forsaken. When we need God the most, as we earthlings surely will in this precarious twenty-first century, we cannot *not* trust. Faith in God is faith that *no matter how bad things get*, somehow or other, it will be all right.

Julian's hazelnut story tells us that God made the earth, God loves it, and God keeps it—three phases of the ever-widening contemplation of the trustworthiness of things, of reality. The hazelnut story is a metaphor of rock-bottom trust that reality is good, that the direction of things is Yes. Everything is loved—the lamb *and* the tiger, the messiness and cost of evolution, all of the contrary events (from any particular perspective), and all of the darkness of life—and everything is "kept" by God (whether it lives or dies). These three moments are the ever-widening contemplation of the world as within God. Each moment is more difficult because it is more inclusive: it is hard to believe that everything is created by God, harder to claim that everything is loved by God, and harder still to trust that everything is kept—protected and cherished—by God. And yet this hope is the one thing needed as we face planetary living in the twenty-first century. "Nature is never spent" and "there lives the deepest freshness deep down things" *because* of the sustaining power and love of God, within whom the earth, our bent world, lives.

If we overcome denial concerning climate change and accept responsibility for it, we face the possibility of incapacitating despair. What Julian and Hopkins—and Christian faith—say is that we should not despair. God "keeps" all things, a new morning springs, the resurrection occurs. In the worst of times, people often say, "All we have is God." Indeed. Here "God" is the thread of hope that desperate people hold on to. God is that scrap of life and goodness still in us. God is what keeps us from giving up. God is not a being, but whatever life or love there is, no matter how small. We hold on to whatever shred of hope is left. It is very small indeed sometimes—but it is enough. "Because the Holy Ghost over the bent / World broods with warm breast and with ah! bright wings."

EPILOGUE

The spring of 2000 was my last semester at Vanderbilt Divinity School after thirty years of teaching. I was selling my house and leaving my children and grandchildren, as well as my country and the job I loved, in order to join my partner in Vancouver, British Columbia. All of this change was disorienting and difficult, but most difficult of all was the death of my wonderful ninety-five-year-old mother. Moreover, I was ill with a then-undiagnosed immune disease that made me constantly tired and prone to respiratory infections. It was a challenging time for me personally, and I had many dark days.

But in the backyard of my house in Nashville was a cherry tree, a thing of rare beauty. I wrote about it in my journal:

> March 19, 2000
> My cherry tree is in full bloom and it is raining—a good, solid, penetrating rain that all the wonderful new buds need. It is Sunday; I am alone, still under the influence of an awful cold, but happy to have a quiet day.
>
> I look at that cherry tree and feel "touched by God." It is a glorious thing and tells of God's glory. Only a cherry tree, *this* cherry tree, can tell of the particular aspect of divine beauty that it alone embodies. It "incarnates" God (as each and every creature and thing does), but in its own special way. There is only one Jesus of Nazareth, but there is also only one cherry tree in the backyard of 3703 Meadowbrook Avenue, Nashville, Tennessee. We are all touched by God, stamped and sealed with some aspect of God. What

a different and wonderful way to understand reality: everything is itself *as* it tells of God. The delicate, irregular limbs and blossoms of this cherry tree, swaying in the breeze, shimmering in the sun: a hymn to God's glory in every twig.

God is not far off, but the near God, nearer to me than my own breath. God is in the cherry tree—oh, yes, especially in my cherry tree! Every time I look at that beautiful creature, I see it shouting out the glory of God. It would not be so beautiful, or so transparent to God, if it were not for the breeze. The filmy white blossoms on the irregular, fragile limbs move in the wind, in the breath of the Holy Spirit, calling me to deeper appreciation of its loveliness. It is saying, "See me speak of God, of a tiny bit of the divine glory, the bit that I can image." I *do* see and I thank you, my cherry tree, for telling me of God. I wish I might do the same. Can any of us be as fine an image of God as a cherry tree?

Few of us can be as fine an image of God as that cherry tree. But each of us is called to be, to do, what we can. During these past eight years since writing *Life Abundant*, I have come to believe that each of us reflects a unique aspect of God's glory—and it is this that we are called to become. We are not expected to save the world or become someone or something else: just ourselves. We become ourselves by acknowledging our radical dependence on God and on our planet: we find our place to be within God, and with and for other creatures. This is who we are. Freed from having to save ourselves or our world, we rest in God, whose body, the world, supports, delights, and calls for our help. To give this help, we have a place in which to stand: within God for the earth. And now we can get to work.

NOTES

Introduction

1. Sallie McFague, *Life Abundant: Rethinking Theology and Economy for a Planet in Peril* (Minneapolis: Fortress Press, 2000).

2. Gerard Manley Hopkins, *Poems and Prose of Gerard Manley Hopkins* (London: Penguin, 1953), 27.

Chapter 1

1. Al Gore, *An Inconvenient Truth: The Planetary Emergency of Global Warming and What We Can Do about It* (New York: Rodale, 2006), 100–101.

2. A few of the many good Web sites on climate change include the following: UN Intergovernmental Panel on Climate Change (www.ipcc.ch); Forum on Religion and Ecology (www.environment.harvard.edu/religion); Earth Charter and Climate Change (www.earthcharterinaction.org.climate); International Society for Religion, Nature, and Culture (www.religionandnature.com); Yale Forestry and Environmental Studies Project on Climate Change (www.environment.yale.edu. climate); and Worldwatch Institute (www.worldwatch.org).

3. See the IPCC Web site, www.ipcc.ch.

4. Tim Flannery, *The Weather Makers: How We Are Changing the Climate and What It Means for Life on Earth* (New York: HarperCollins, 2005), 246.

5. Gore, *Inconvenient Truth*, 263–64.

6. Quoted in ibid., 260–61.

7. Quoted in "The Politics behind the Peace Prize, "*New York Times*, October 14, 2007.

8. Intergovermental Panel on Climate Change, 2007, http://www.ipcc.ch (February 2008).

9. Quoted in Flannery, *Weather Makers*, 166.

10. As reported in Randy Boswell, "Northwest Passage is Wide Open for Shipping," *Vancouver Sun*, April 29, 2007, A5.

11. Corinne Le Quere commenting on a paper from the Proceedings of the National Academy of Sciences, published online October 22, 2007, quoted in *Globe and Mail*, October 23, 2007, A14. See also the fourth UN Global Environment Outlook (2007) for its most comprehensive survey of the environment, a survey that reveals an accelerated rate of climate forcing and resource deterioration.

12. Elizabeth Kolbert, *Field Notes from a Catastrophe: Man, Nature, and Climate Change* (New York: Bloomsbury, 2006), 86.

13. For an explanation of this complex phenomenon, see "Common Misconceptions about Abrupt Climate Change," *Woods Hole Oceanographic Institution*, February 15, 2008, http://www.whoi.edu/page.do?pid=12455&tid=282&cid=10149#ocean_1 (February 2008).

14. Kolbert, *Field Notes*, 107–8.

15. See Robert B. Gagosian, "Abrupt Climate Change: Should We Be Worried?" *Woods Hole Oceanographic Institution*, February 15, 2008, http://www.whoi.edu/page.do?pid =12455&tid=282&cid=9986 (February 2008).

16. Donald Perovich, quoted in Kolbert, *Field Notes*, 34.

17. Flannery, *Weather Makers*, 12–13.

18. Ibid., 23.

19. Gore, *Inconvenient Truth*, 58.

20. Ibid., 132.

21. George Monbiot, *Heat: How to Stop the Planet from Burning* (Toronto: Doubleday, 2006), 22.

22. Ibid., 173.

23. Ibid., 22.

24. Ibid., 187.

25. Gore, *Inconvenient Truth*, 232–33.

26. United Nations, *Human Development Report 1998* (New York: Oxford University Press, 1998), 2.

27. Flannery, *Weather Makers*, 78–79.

28. Intergovernmental Panel on Climate Change, "Climate Change 2007: Climate Change Impacts, Adaptation and Vulnerability; Summary for Policymakers."

29. Quoted in Scott Simpson, "World's Poorest Will Be Hardest Hit by Climate Change," *Vancouver Sun*, April 7, 2007, A4.

30. Quoted in Andrew Revkin, "The Climate Divide: Wealth and Poverty, Drought and Flood: Reports from 4 Fronts in the War on Warming," *New York Times*, April 3, 2007, D4.

31. Quoted in Andrew Revkin, "Poorest Nations Will Bear Brunt as World Warms," *New York Times*, April 1, 2007, 6.

32. Ibid.

33. As quoted in Revkin, "The Climate Divide," D4.

34. Quoted in Jeff Mason, "Poorest of the Poor Will Be Hit Hardest," *Globe and Mail*, April 7, 2007, A3.

35. Flannery, *Weather Makers*, 170.

36. Intergovernmental Panel on Climate Change, "Climate Change 2007: Mitigation of Climate Change; Summary for Policymakers."

37. Monbiot, *Heat*, 213.

38. Ibid.

39. Ibid., xxi.

40. Ibid., xiii.

41. Ibid., xxv.

42. Ibid., 56.

Chapter 2

1. Pierre Teilhard de Chardin, "Cosmic Life," in *Writings in Time of War*, trans. Rene Hague (New York: Harper & Row, 1968), 13–71.

2. "We have to be catholic, that is to say, not bound by so much as a thread to any created thing, unless it be to creation in its totality." Simone Weil, *Waiting for God*, trans. Emma Craufurd (New York: Harper & Row, 1951), 98.

3. Ibid.

4. For further elaboration, see Sallie McFague, *Life Abundant: Rethinking Theology and Economy for a Planet in Peril* (Minneapolis: Fortress Press, 2000), ch. 5.

5. See George S. Hendry, *Theology of Nature* (Philadelphia: Westminster, 1980), ch. 1.

6. For further discussion of this point, see Sallie McFague, *The Body of God: An Ecological Theology* (Minneapolis: Fortress Press, 1993), ch. 2.

7. For further elaboration, see McFague, *Life Abundant*, ch. 8.

8. For discussion of this point, see ibid., chs. 4 and 5.

9. For a fuller treatment, see ch. 5.

10. John Dominic Crossan, *Jesus: A Revolutionary Biography* (San Francisco: HarperSanFrancisco, 1994), 66*ff*.

11. Robert Costanza et al., *An Introduction to Ecological Economics* (Boca Raton, Fla.: St. Lucie, 1997), 179.

Chapter 3

1. This chapter, originally a class lecture, lacks the usual number of endnotes for publication. I believe much of what I say here is "common knowledge," and while I could reference it, doing so seems superfluous in light of the introductory nature of much of the material. I will, however, list a range of sources that make points similar to the ones in this chapter. Ian Barbour, *Religion in an Age of Science*, vol. 1 (San Francisco: Harper & Row, 1990); Thomas Berry, *The Dream of the Earth* (San Francisco: Sierra Club Books, 1988); Charles Birch, William Eakin, and Jay B. McDaniel, eds., *Liberating Life: Contemporary Approaches to Ecological Theology* (Maryknoll, N.Y.: Orbis, 1991); Richard C. Foltz, ed., *Worldviews, Religion, and the Environment: A Global Anthology* (Belmont, Calif.: Wadsworth/Learning, 2003); Al Gore, *Earth in the Balance: Ecology and the Human Spirit* (Boston: Houghton Mifflin, 2003); David G. Hallman, ed., *Ecotheology: Voices from South and North* (Maryknoll, N.Y.: Orbis, 1994); Dieter Hessel and Rosemary Radford Ruether, eds., *Christianity and Ecology: Seeking the Well-Being of Earth and Humans* (Cambridge: Harvard University Press, 2000); Carolyn Merchant, *Radical Ecology: The Search for a Livable World* (New York: Routledge, 1992); A. R. Peacocke, *Creation and the World of Science* (Oxford: Clarendon, 1979); Larry L. Rasmussen, *Earth Community, Earth Ethics* (Maryknoll, N.Y.: Orbis, 1996); Rosemary Radford Ruether, *Gaia and God: An Ecofeminist Theology of Earth Healing* (San Francisco: Harper & Row, 1992); David Suzuki, *The Sacred Balance: Rediscovering Our Place in Nature* (Vancouver: Douglas & McIntyre, 1997); Edward O. Wilson, *The Diversity of Life* (New York: W. W. Norton, 1992).

2. Wallace Stevens, *Opus Posthumous: Poems, Plays, Prose*, ed. Milton J. Bates (New York: Vintage, 1990), (New York: Vintage, 1990), 163.

3. Ibid.

4. See George S. Hendry, *Theology of Nature* (Philadelphia: Westminster, 1980), ch. 1.

5. Thich Nhat Hanh, *The Sun My Heart: From Mindfulness to Insight Meditation* (Berkeley, Calif.: Parallax, 1988), 90.

6. Berry, *The Dream of the Earth*, 47–48.

Chapter 4

1. Annie Dillard, *Pilgrim at Tinker Creek: A Mystical Excursion into the Natural World* (New York: Bantam, 1975), 2, 12.

2. First Vatican Council, "Dogmatic Constitution concerning Catholic Faith," in *The Sources of Catholic Dogma*, ed. Heinrich Denzinger, trans. Roy J. Defarrari (St. Louis: B. Herder, 1957), 443.

3. First Vatican Council, the Basilica of Saint Peter, Vatican City, Italy, 1869–1870.

4. There is a large literature covering a range of scholarship on divine intervention and design, from the current "creationists" with their literal interpretation of Genesis to nuanced accounts of the "anthropic principle" (the proposal that the existence of creatures as complex as human beings could not have occurred apart from a Designer). For a thoughtful set of reflections on this issue, see *Evidence of Purpose: Scientists Discover the Creator*, ed. John Marks Templeton (New York: Continuum, 1994).

5. Augustine, *Confessions* 1.2, trans. F. J. Sheed (Indianapolis: Hackett, 1993), 3–4.

6. See Sallie McFague, *The Body of God: An Ecological Theology* (Minneapolis: Fortress Press, 1993), for an interpretation of this model.

7. This, of course, is the Augustinian view of evil, which, while having Platonic and idealistic overtones, nonetheless attempts to refute any contemporary rebirths of Manichaeanism: that evil is an ontological force comparable to God, to good. One sees inklings of this view emerge in the recent American foreign policy rhetoric of the "axis of evil." An Augustinian view of evil puts responsibility squarely on human shoulders—not on the "enemy," nor fate, nor another god. It also underscores that the source of all goodness and the power for goodness is the one reality, God.

8. H. Richard Niebuhr, *The Responsible Self: An Essay in Christian Moral Philosophy* (New York: Harper & Row, 1963), 175.

Chapter 5

1. This chapter is a summary of significant points in my book *Life Abundant: Rethinking Theology and Economy for a Planet in Peril* (Minneapolis: Fortress Press, 2000), esp. chs. 4 and 5.

2. See George S. Hendry, *Theology of Nature* (Philadelphia: Westminster, 1980), ch. 1.

3. For a fuller treatment of metaphors and models, see Sallie McFague, *Models of God: Theology for an Ecological, Nuclear Age* (Minneapolis: Fortress Press, 1987); also see ch. 6 of this book.

4. Lynn White Jr., "The Historical Roots of Our Ecological Crisis," *Science* 155 (March 10, 1967): 1203–7.

5. Marcus Borg describes this well: "A root image is a fundamental 'picture' of reality. Perhaps most often called a 'world-view,' it consists of our most taken-for-granted assumptions about what is possible. . . . Very importantly, a root image not only provides a model of reality, but also shapes our perception and our thinking, operating almost unconsciously within us as a

dim background affecting all of our seeing and thinking. A root image thus functions as both an image and a lens: it is a picture of reality which becomes a lens through which we see reality." Marcus J. Borg, *Jesus in Contemporary Scholarship* (Valley Forge, Pa.: Trinity Press, International, 1994), 127.

6. See ch. 3 of this book for a fuller treatment.

7. The literature on the neoclassical economic model and its alternative—what I am calling the ecological economic model—is large and growing. Some of the works I found most helpful are as follows: Lester R. Brown et al., *State of the World: A Worldwatch Institute Report on Progress toward a Sustainable Society* (New York: W. W. Norton, issued annually); Robert Costanza et al., *An Introduction to Ecological Economics* (Boca Raton, Fla.: St. Lucie, 1997); David A. Crocker and Toby Linden, eds., *Ethics of Consumption: The Good Life, Justice, and Global Stewardship* (Lanham, Md.: Rowman & Littlefield, 1998); Herman E. Daly and John B. Cobb Jr., *For the Common Good: Redirecting the Economy toward Community, the Environment, and a Sustainable Future*, 2nd ed. (Boston: Beacon, 1994); Herman E. Daly, *Beyond Growth: The Economics of Sustainable Development* (Boston: Beacon, 1996); Neva R. Goodwin, Frank Ackerman, and David Kirion, eds., *The Consumer Society* (Washington, D.C.: Island, 1997); Steven C. Hackett, *Environmental and Natural Resources Economics: Theory, Policy and the Sustainable Society* (Armonk, N.Y.: E. E. Sharpe, 1998); Larry L. Rasmussen, *Earth Community, Earth Ethics* (Maryknoll, N.Y.: Orbis, 1996); Joerg Rieger, ed., *Liberating the Future: God, Mammon, and Theology* (Minneapolis: Fortress Press, 1998); *United Nations Human Development Report* (New York: Oxford University Press, issued annually); United Nations Environment Programme (UNEP), "Millennium Ecosystem Assessment Reports," *Millennium Ecosystem Assessment*, 2005, http://www.millenniumassessment.org/en/Index. aspx (February 2008); Michael Zweig, ed., *Religion and Economic Justice* (Philadelphia: Temple University Press, 1991), 6.

8. The evidence supporting this claim would take considerable space to lay out. Suffice it to say here that both the born-again Christian and New Age versions of popular religion do so; the American Declaration of Independence's "life, liberty, and the pursuit of happiness" does; and Adam Smith's description of the human being as a creature of insatiable greed makes a significant contribution. All focus on the rights, desires, and needs of *individuals*.

9. Milton Friedman's distinction between "positive" and "normative" economics is typical: "Normative economics is speculative and personal, a matter of values and preferences that are beyond science. Economics as a science, as a tool for understanding and predication, must be based solely on positive economics which 'is in principle independent of any particular

ethical position or normative judgments.'" Milton Friedman, *Essays in Positive Economics* (Chicago: University of Chicago Press, 1953), 4.

10. Hackett, *Environmental and Natural Resources Economics*, 33.

11. See Daly, *Beyond Growth*, 50*ff.*

12. Janet N. Abramowitz, "Valuing Nature's Services," in *State of the World 1997: A Worldwide Institute Report on Progress toward a Sustainable Society*, ed. Lester R. Brown et al. (New York: W. W. Norton, 1997).

13. Ibid., 109.

14. If all contemporary understandings of Christ should be grounded in historical judgments about Jesus of Nazareth—if there should be continuity between the Jesus of history and the Christ of faith—then we need to see if the ecological economic context is an appropriate one for interpreting Christ and Christian discipleship for the twenty-first century. I am not suggesting that a Christian's faith is based on the state of historical Jesus research at any particular time; nonetheless, Christianity has always claimed continuity with its founder. Recent research, which has moved out of narrow church contexts of interpretation to sociological, cultural, and political ones of first-century Mediterranean society, has reached a remarkable consensus on some broad outlines of Jesus' life; most notably that he was a social revolutionary opposed to the structures of domination and domestication of his day. This consensus is expressed in different ways by New Testament scholars such as E. P. Sanders, Burton Mack, Elisabeth Schüssler Fiorenza, Marcus Borg, John Dominic Crossan, and Richard Horsley. For an overview of the scholarship, see Borg, *Jesus in Contemporary Scholarship*.

15. John Dominic Crossan, *Jesus: A Revolutionary Biography* (San Francisco: HarperSanFrancisco, 1994).

16. Ibid., 73–74.

17. Ibid., 68.

18. Ibid., 113.

19. See ibid., 79–81.

20. See letter of April 30, 1944, in Dietrich Bonhoeffer, *Letters and Papers from Prison* (London: Collins, 1960).

Chapter 6

1. John D. Caputo, *On Religion* (New York: Routledge, 2001), 140–41.

2. Ibid., 28.

3. Simone Weil, *First and Last Notebooks*, trans. Richard Rees (London: Oxford University Press), 104.

4. Annie Dillard, *Pilgrim at Tinker Creek: A Mystical Excursion into the Natural World* (New York: Bantam, 1975), 279; quoted in Dorothee Soelle, *The Silent Cry: Mysticism and Resistance*, trans. Barbara and Martin Rumscheidt (Minneapolis: Fortress Press, 2001), 91.

5. *Poems and Prose of Gerard Manley Hopkins* (London: Penguin, 1953), 27; E. O. Wilson, *Biophilia* (Cambridge: Harvard Univ. Press, 1984); Stephen Jay Gould, *Wonderful Life: The Burgess Shale and the Nature of History* (New York: W.W. Norton, 1989).

6. Dillard, *Pilgrim at Tinker Creek*, 8.

7. See John D. Caputo and Michael J. Scanlon, eds., *God, the Gift, and Postmodernism* (Bloomington: Indiana University Press, 1999), introduction and chs. 1 and 2.

8. See Michael J. Scanlon, "A Deconstruction of Religion: On Derrida and Rahner," in Caputo and Scanlon, *God, the Gift, and Postmodernism*, 228.

9. Caputo, *On Religion*, 115.

10. For an interesting discussion on this issue of onto-theology versus praise, see Merold Westphal, "Overcoming Onto-theology," in Caputo and Scanlon, *God, the Gift and Postmodernism*, 150, 164.

11. Catherine Keller writes, "Might the 'in' of panentheism begin to designate *creation as incarnation?*" Catherine Keller, *Face of the Deep: A Theology of Becoming* (New York: Routledge, 2003), 219. While Keller's perspective is more clearly Whiteheadian than mine, there are nonetheless many points of overlap between her understanding of "apophatic panentheism" and my view of the world as God's body. In both, as Keller puts it, "if the incarnation is co-extensive with the body of creation, then might not all matter—and not only the baby's skin, the lover's eye, the winter sunrise—exude an incandescence of the deep?" (221).

12. Jacques Derrida, "White Mythology: Metaphor in the Text of Philosophy," *New Literary History* 6 (1974): 41–42.

13. Ibid., 11.

14. Ibid., 70.

15. See Philip Wheelwright, *The Burning Fountain: A Study in the Language of Symbolism* (Bloomington: Indiana University Press, 1968), 86.

16. Westphal, "Overcoming Onto-theology," 150.

17. Ibid., 164.

18. Derrida, "White Mythology," 11.

19. See Thomas Carlson's statement on the subordination of religious (imagistic) to philosophical (conceptual) thought in Hegel: "The annulment of time, the death of death, and the correlative conception of love in terms of infinite self-consciousness—all occur within a framework that subordinates religious to philosophical thought. From the Hegelian perspective,

that subordination is necessitated by the inadequacy of the religious, or representational, form of thought with regard to the philosophical, or wholly conceptual, form." Thomas A. Carlson, *Indiscretion: Finitude and the Naming of God* (Chicago: University of Chicago Press, 1999), 241.

20. Derrida, "White Mythology," 74.

21. See Sallie McFague, *Speaking in Parables: A Study in Metaphor and Theology* (Minneapolis: Fortress Press, 1975).

22. David Tracy, "Fragments: The Spiritual Situation of Our Times," *God, the Gift, and Postmodernism*, 179.

23. See Sallie McFague, *The Body of God: An Ecological Theology* (Minneapolis: Fortress Press, 1993).

24. Tracy, "Fragments," 172.

25. See, for instance, David Tracy, *The Analogical Imagination: Christian Theology and the Culture of Pluralism* (New York: Crossroad, 1981).

26. John D. Caputo, "What Do I Love When I Love My God? Deconstruction and Radical Orthodoxy," in *Questioning God*, ed. John D. Caputo, Mark Dooley, and Michael J. Scanlon (Bloomington: Indiana University Press, 2001), 304.

27. John D. Caputo, *More Radical Hermeneutics: On Not Knowing Who We Are* (Bloomington: Indiana University Press, 2000), 7.

28. Ibid., 200.

29. Ibid., 207.

30. Ibid., 213.

31. Weil, *First and Last Notebooks*, 307.

32. Ibid., 104.

33. Ibid., 111; Simone Weil, *Waiting for God*, trans. Emma Craufurd (London: Routledge, Kegan Paul, 1951), 197.

34. Weil, *First and Last Notebooks*, 284.

35. See Pierre Teilhard de Chardin, *How I Believe*, trans. Rene Hague (New York: Harper & Row, 1969).

36. Francis Schüssler Fiorenza, "Being, Subjectivity, Otherness: The Idols of God," in Caputo, Dooley, and Scanlon, *Questioning God*, 352.

37. Richard Kearney, "The God Who May Be," in Caputo, Dooley, and Scanlon, *Questioning God*, 169.

38. Weil, *Waiting for God*, 161.

39. Weil, *First and Last Notebooks*, 83.

40. See Sallie McFague, *Super, Natural Christians: How We Should Love Nature* (Minneapolis: Fortress Press, 1997), ch. 3.

41. The model of the world as God's body is an old and widely prevalent one; see McFague, *Body of God*, chs. 2 and 3.

42. See, for example, A. R. Peacocke's discussion of female birth imagery as a metaphor for divine creation: "Mammalian females . . . create within themselves and the growing embryo resides within the female body and this is a proper corrective to the masculine picture—it is an analogy of God creating the world within herself. . . . God creates a world that is, in principle and in origin, other than him/herself but creates it, the world, within him/herself." A. R. Peacocke, *Creation and the World of Science* (Oxford: Clarendon, 1979), 142.

43. Dorothee Soelle, *The Silent Cry: Mysticism and Resistance*, trans. Barbara and Martin Rumscheidt (Minneapolis: Fortress Press, 2001), 302.

44. Caputo, *On Religion*, 137.

45. Edith Wyschogrod, *Saints and Postmodernism: Revisioning Moral Philosophy* (Chicago: University of Chicago Press, 1990), 72.

46. Weil, *First and Last Notebooks*, 286.

47. See the discussion of the loving and the arrogant eye in McFague *Super, Natural Christians*, chs. 4 and 5.

48. John Woolman, *The Journal and a Plea for the Poor* (New York: Corinth, 1961), 43.

49. Ibid., 214.

50. Paul Lachance, "Mysticism and Social Transformation according to the Franciscan Way," *Mysticism and Social Transformation*, ed. Janet K. Ruffing (Syracuse, N.Y.: Syracuse University Press, 2001), 69.

51. Quoted in Murray Bodo, *The Way of St. Francis: The Challenge of Franciscan Spirituality for Everyone* (New York: Doubleday, 1985), 51.

52. Weil, *First and Last Notebooks*, 212.

53. Soelle, *Silent Cry*, 141.

54. Wyschogrod, *Saints and Postmodernism*, xxii.

55. Ibid., 50–52.

56. Weil, *First and Last Notebooks*, 94, 312.

57. Caputo, *On Religion*, 141.

58. E. E. Cummings, "I Thank You God for Most This Amazing Day," *E. E. Cummings: Complete Poems 1904–1962*, rev. ed. (New York: Liveright Publishing, 2004).

59. Erich Heller, *The Disinherited Mind: Essays in Modern German Literature and Thought* (Cleveland, Ohio: World, 1961), 211.

Chapter 7

1. Michael Pollan, *The Omnivore's Dilemma: A Natural History of Four Meals* (New York: Penguin, 2006), 10.

2. Catherine Keller, "Introduction: Grounding Theory: Earth in Religion and Philosophy," in *Ecospirit: Religion, Philosophy, and the Earth,* ed. Laurel Kearns and Catherine Keller (New York: Fordham University Press, 2007), 7.

3. Edward Soja notes the history of these terms: "...Hegelian and Marxian notions of 'second Nature,' a socialized world created from a pristine 'first' Nature but increasingly separate and distinct, subject to its own laws and development." Edward Soja, "Seeing Nature Spatially" (paper presented at "Without Nature: A New Condition for Theology," University of Chicago Divinity School conference, October 26–28, 2006), 2–3. A more down-to-earth definition of "second nature" can be seen in the title of Michael Pollan's book *Second Nature: A Gardener's Education* (New York: Dell, 1991). Here it is not the city as a whole that is second nature, but city gardens in contrast to nature untouched by human hands.

4. Langdon Gilkey, *Nature, Reality, and the Sacred: The Nexus of Science and Religion* (Minneapolis: Fortress Press, 1993), 178.

5. Ibid., 179.

6. Ibid.

7. Ibid.

8. Soja, "Seeing Nature Spatially," 13.

9. Ibid.

10. T. J. Gorringe, *A Theology of the Built Environment: Justice, Empowerment, Redemption* (Cambridge: Cambridge University Press, 2002), 23.

11. Linda Stark, ed., *State of the World 2007: Our Urban Future* (New York: W. W. Norton, 2007).

12. Ibid., preface, xxiii.

13. Ibid., 93.

14. Ibid., 91.

15. Ibid., xx.

16. Quoted in Soja, "Seeing Nature Spatially," 13.

17. See www.earthcharter.org. "The Earth Charter," Appendix in Richard C. Foltz, ed. *Worldviews, Religion, and the Environment: A Global Anthropology* (Belmont, CA: Thompson/Wadsworth, 2003), 592.

18. Pollan, *Omnivore's Dilemma*, 17.

19. Ibid., 9.

20. Ibid., 10.

21. Ibid., 411.

22. J. Cook, "Environmentally Benign Architecture," in *Global Warming and the Built Environment*, ed. R. Samuels and D. Prasad (London: Spon, 1994), 143.

23. Peter H. Raven, "The Sustainability of the Earth: Our Common Responsibility," (paper presented at "Without Nature: A New Condition for Theology," University of Chicago Divinity School conference, October 26–28, 2006), 4–5.

24. United Nations Environment Programme (UNEP), "Living beyond Our Means: Natural Assets and Human Well-Being," *Millennium Ecosystem Assessment: Statement of the Board*, 2005, http://www.maweb.org/en/BoardStatement.aspx (February 2008).

25. Ibid., 17.

26. Ibid., 5.

27. Ibid., 6.

28. Ibid., 3.

29. Ibid., 5.

30. David Harvey, *Spaces of Hope* (Berkeley: University of California Press, 2000), 220.

31. Raven, "Sustainability of the Earth," 25.

32. See S. Kjellberg, *Urban Eco Theology* (Utrecht: International Books, 2000), 46.

33. Carolyn Merchant, *The Death of Nature: Women, Ecology and the Scientific Revolution* (San Francisco: Harper & Row, 1983).

34. Harvey, *Spaces of Hope*, 97.

35. For further elaboration, see Sallie McFague, *The Body of God: An Ecological Theology* (Minneapolis: Fortress Press, 1993).

36. For discussion of the epistemological and theological role of metaphor and model, see Sallie McFague, *Metaphorical Theology: Models of God in Religious Language* (Minneapolis: Fortress Press, 1982), and *Models of God: Theology for an Ecological, Nuclear Age* (Minneapolis: Fortress Press, 1987).

37. Jacques Derrida, "White Mythology: Metaphor in the Text of Philosophy," *New Literary History* 6 (1974): 41–42.

38. For further elaboration of this and related issues, see Sallie McFague, *Life Abundant: Rethinking Theology and Economy for a Planet in Peril* (Minneapolis: Fortress Press, 2000).

39. David Harvey, *Justice, Nature and the Geography of Difference* (Oxford: Blackwell, 1996), 429.

40. Stark, *State of the World 2007*, 14.

41. The natural theology tradition of Roman Catholicism, epitomized by Thomas Aquinas, sees creation as a reflection of God. It is not just human beings who are made in the image of God; rather, all creatures are. As Thomas Aquinas expresses it: "But creatures cannot attain to any perfect likeness of God so long as they are confined to one species of creatures; because, since

the cause exceeds the effect in a composite and manifold way. . . . Multiplicity, therefore, and variety, was needful in the creation, to the end that the perfect likeness of God might be found in things according to their measure." Quoted in Arthur O. Lovejoy, *The Great Chain of Being: A Study in the History of an Idea* (Cambridge: Harvard University Press, 1933), 76.

42. Iris Murdoch, "The Sublime and the Good," *Chicago Review* 13 (Autumn 1950): 51.

43. "We are seeing the urban future and it is slums—slums on a frightening scale." Stephen Hume, *Vancouver Sun*, June 21, 2006, A17. See the United Nations report "State of the World's Cities: Globalization and Urban Culture, 2004–2005" *Findarticles.com*, n.d., http://findarticles.com/p/articles/mi_m1309/is_4_41/ai_n13801011 (February 2008).

44. Report of the Third Session of the World Urban Forum, June 19–23, 2006, Vancouver, British Columbia, *World Urban Forum*, 2006, http://www.wuf3-fum3 .ca/Report/en/index.html (February 2008).

45. See, for instance, George F. R. Ellis, "Kenosis as a Unifying Theme for Life and Cosmology," Keith Ward, "Cosmos and Kenosis," and Jürgen Moltmann, "God's Kenosis in the Creation and the Consummation of the World," in *The Work of Love: Creation and Kenosis*, ed. John Polkinghorne (Grand Rapids: Eerdmans, 2001).

46. See *The Emptying God: A Buddhist-Jewish-Christian Conversation*, ed. John B. Cobb Jr. and Christopher Ives (New York: Orbis, 1998).

47. Edith Wyschogrod, *Saints and Postmodernism: Revisioning Moral Philosophy* (Chicago: University of Chicago Press, 1990), xxii.

48. See J. P. Little, "Simone Weil's Concept of Decreation," in *Simone Weil's Philosophy of Culture: Readings Toward a Divine Humanity*, ed. Richard H. Bell (Cambridge: Cambridge University Press, 1993).

Chapter 8

1. Iris Murdoch, "The Sublime and the Good," *Chicago Review* 13 (Autumn 1959): 51.

2. John Woolman, *The Journal of John Woolman* (New York: Corinth, 1961), 8.

3. See Andrew Michael Flescher, *Heroes, Saints, and Ordinary Morality* (Washington, D.C.: Georgetown University Press, 2003).

4. Quoted in ibid., 186.

5. Nellie McClung, "Ecotherapy News, Autumn 2006," *Ecotherapy News*, 2006, http://thoughtoffering.blogs.com/ecotherapy/2006/09/index.html (February 2008).

6. Quoted in "Emmanuel College Newsletter" (Toronto: Autumn 2004).

7. Gustavo Gutierrez, *A Theology of Liberation: History, Politics, and Salvation*, trans. Sister Caridad and John Eagleson (Maryknoll, N.Y.: Orbis, 1971), 201.

8. Dorothee Soelle, *The Silent Cry: Mysticism and Resistance* (Minneapolis: Fortress Press, 2001), 255.

9. Dorothy Day, *The Long Loneliness: The Autobiography of Dorothy Day* (New York: Curtis Books, 1952).

10. Flescher, *Heroes, Saints, and Ordinary Morality*, 316.

11. Quoted in ibid., 311.

Chapter 9

1. John Pick, ed., *A Hopkins Reader* (New York: Oxford University Press, 1953), 13.

2. Sallie McFague, *Models of God: Theology for an Ecological, Nuclear Age* (Minneapolis: Fortress Press, 1987), 169–71. However, in my next book, *The Body of God* (Minneapolis: Fortress Press, 1993), I realize the importance of the model: see pp. 141*ff.*

3. Christopher Devlin, ed., *The Sermons and Devotional Writings of Gerard Manley Hopkins* (Oxford: Oxford University Press, 1959), 195.

4. Gerard Manley Hopkins, "The Blessed Virgin Compared to the Air We Breathe" (1883), in Pick, *Hopkins Reader*, 21.

5. *Random House Webster's College Dictionary* (New York: Random House, 1997), 1053.

6. Julian of Norwich, *Revelation of Love*, ed. and trans. John Skinner (New York: Doubleday Image, 1997), 10–11.

7. Ibid., 60.

ACKNOWLEDGMENTS

I am thankful to my students at the Vancouver School of Theology who suffered through lecture versions of these chapters in several courses. I am especially indebted to a class on Climate Change and Christian Faith in the fall of 2007 and the students who worked through the book in draft. I list their names here in appreciation: Allan Aicken, Wes Buch, Jim Cooney, Louise Cummings, Nan Geer, Judith Hardcastle, Beatrice Marovich, Sharon Proske, Elizabeth Rathbun, Geoff Salomons, Martha Schattman, Emilie Smith, and Paul Thiessen.

I would not have written this book without Michael West. I did not think I had another book in me, but he persuaded me otherwise. He has been far more than an editor or even an inspiration: he has been a partner. From the earliest versions of the ms., Michael's insight, direction, questions, critique, and support have buoyed me onwards and given me a path to follow. I wavered between dedicating the book to him or to my granddaughters. I chose the latter because they represent the future of the book's concern—climate change—but if it is possible to have a secret or second dedication, it goes to Michael, with my deepest gratitude.

I also wish to acknowledge the good folks at Fortress Press, my longtime publisher. They have kept my books in print and it has been a pleasure to work with them and especially with Timothy W. Larson on the present book.

I want also to acknowledge that many other people have read and commented on parts of the ms., and I thank them anonymously. I must, however, mention the steady support and insightful critique of my partner, Janet Cawley, who is the delight of my life.

I am also grateful that, over the last several years, I have been able to explore the ideas formulated in this book in many presentations and publications. Although the ideas and formulations have changed somewhat for this volume, I want especially to acknowledge publications of my prior work in these related publications:

"The Church is Ecological" in William Madges and Michael J. Daley, eds. *The Many Marks of the Church* (New London, CT: Twenty-Third Publications, 2006), 124–27.

"Is God in Charge? Creation and Providence" in William C. Placher, ed., *Essentials of Christian Theology* (Louisville: Westminster John Knox Press, 2003), 101–116.

"God's Household: Christianity, Economics, and Planetary Living" in Paul F. Knitter and Chandra Muzaffar, eds., *Subverting Greed: Religious Perspectives on the Global Economy* (Maryknoll, NY: Orbis Books and Cambridge: Boston Research Center for the 21st Century, 2002). 119–136.

"Intimations of Transcendence: Praise and Compassion" in John E. Caputo and Michael J. Scanlon, eds. *Transcendence and Beyond: A Postmodern Inquiry* (Bloomington, IN: Indiana University Press, 2007), 151–168.

INDEX